GOD SAID
TO OVER 3000
PROMISES

NO MATTER HOW MANY PROMISES GOD HAS MADE, THEY ARE YES AND AMEN IN CHRIST

CLINT BYARS

DEDICATION

This book is dedicated to the members of Forward Church. You inspire me to continually say yes to God. Your heart of compassion toward my family and toward one another is life giving. I pray this resource empowers you to say yes to God because he says yes to you in all of his promises.

CONTENTS

Dedication   iii

Acknowledgments   iv

Introduction   1

Key Promises   3

Identity Promises   7

New Testament Promises   13

Old Testament Promises   55

Why are the Promises
not manifesting in my life?   90

ACKNOWLEDGMENTS

There is only one person to acknowledge, the Lord Jesus himself. Jesus could have come to planet earth, lived a sinless life, died the death we deserved, rose again in total victory, ascended to Heaven and then say to us, 'I've secured salvation for you in the after life, the door is open, I hope you make it to Heaven.'

But he didn't do that. He did all of those things but he also made us great and precious promises so we could be partakers of his divine nature while we are here on this planet. He could have come here, paid for our sin and gone back to Heaven, leaving us alone but he didn't. He gave us his Holy Spirit to help us connect with all of his promises in *this* life.

Thank you Jesus! Thank you for not leaving us alone! Thank you for your great and precious promises! Thank you for giving us a new heart! Thank you for placing your spirit in us! Thank you that your spirit continually reminds us that we are your children! Thank you that you have qualified us to be partakers of the inheritance of the saints in light! Thank you!

INTRODUCTION

There are over 3000 promises from God in the Bible. Look at what the Apostle Paul says about God's promises.

2 Corinthians 1: 19 For the Son of God, Jesus Christ, who was preached among you by me and Silas and Timothy, was not "Yes" and "No," but in him it has always been "Yes." 20 **For no matter how many promises God has made, they are "Yes" in Christ. And so through him the "Amen" is spoken by us to the glory of God.** 21 Now it is God who makes both us and you stand firm in Christ. He anointed us, 22 set his seal of ownership on us, and put his Spirit in our hearts as a deposit, guaranteeing what is to come.

No matter how many promises God has made, they are YES in Christ. Not maybe, not "in the right timing," not after you've preformed properly but in Christ, YES! But WHY has God made those promises available to his children?

2 Peter 1:2 **Grace** and **peace** be multiplied unto you through the knowledge of God, and of Jesus our Lord, 3 According as his divine power **hath given unto us all things that pertain unto life and godliness**, through the knowledge of him that hath called us to glory and virtue: 4 Whereby are given unto us exceeding **great and precious promises: that by these ye might be partakers of the divine nature**, having escaped the corruption that is in the world through lust.

Why the promises? So **you** would be a partaker of God's divine nature, right now, in this life, in this body!

Do you believe the Bible or do you believe your circumstances? Often we feel it's too difficult to muster up courage to try and believe again, but you can rest assured that if you are in Christ through faith, God is seeking to make His promises a reality in your life. You are qualified in Jesus alone. Romans 8 tells us that we are already in Christ if we believe, so being in Christ is not conditional upon your ability to "walk in the spirit." If Christ is in you, you are constantly "in the spirit." Don't let your past or current behavior disqualify you from God's promises and don't be tricked into believing that being "in Christ" is dependent upon your spiritual performance. If you have believed on Jesus as your righteousness, you are in Christ therefore qualified for 2 Corinthians 1:20!

Romans 8:9 But you are not in the flesh but in the Spirit, if indeed the Spirit of God dwells in you. Now if anyone does not have the Spirit of Christ, he is not His.

Do not let your mind jump to the what if's and what about's, as if you can figure out how to get the promises to work, just take a moment to believe God. Take a moment to take God at His word and be persuaded that He desires good things for you and is actively seeking to bring about his good plans to prosper you.

Now let's look at the second part of 2 Corinthians 1:20 "so through Him the "Amen" is spoken by us to the glory of God." Amen means *to establish*. You have a part to play in establishing God's promises in your life, believing AND speaking. We could say it this way, God's promises are established in our lives as we speak.

I am not talking about trying to persuade God to give us things through fervent prayer, I'm talking about coming into agreement with who God has revealed Himself to be, what He said in His Word and making sure our words line up with that. When was the last time you spoke the truth of God over your situation? There are over 3000 promises in the Bible, I'm sure you can do some digging and find at least one that applies to your situation. As you speak God's truth over your situation, be sure that you are convinced of His love for you in that specific area. You may have tried many times to believe God in that situation but **He hasn't given up on you yet, don't give up on Him**. You can trust Him. He is your Heavenly Father who loves you dearly and it's His good pleasure to give you His Kingdom.

KEY PROMISES

Keep in mind as you read through these passages that all of God's promises are yes and amen **for you**. These promises are for your life, **today**. Everything God has for you is freely available because of Christ and they manifest in your life by grace through faith toward God. He has good plans for you, believe and walk in his promises. Open your heart to feel the truth of each of these passages. Meditate on them until your emotions change and match the truth expressed in each passage.

1 Corinthians 15:3 For I delivered to you as of first importance what I also received: that Christ died for our sins in accordance with the Scriptures, 4 that he was buried, that he was raised on the third day in accordance with the Scriptures 57 But thanks be to God, who gives us the victory through our Lord Jesus Christ.

Acts 2:38 Peter replied, "Repent and be baptized, every one of you, in the name of Jesus Christ for the forgiveness of your sins. And you will receive the gift of the Holy Spirit. 39 The promise is for you and your children and for all who are far off—for all whom the Lord our God will call."

John 10:27 My sheep listen to my voice; I know them, and they follow me. 28 I give them eternal life, and they shall never perish; no one will snatch them out of my hand.

Colossians 1:12 Giving thanks unto the Father, which hath made us meet to be partakers of the inheritance of the saints in light: 13 Who hath delivered us from the power of darkness, and hath translated us into the kingdom of his dear Son: 14 In whom we have redemption through his blood, even the forgiveness of sins:

Colossians 1:19 For it pleased the Father that in him should all fulness dwell; 20 And, having made peace through the blood of his cross, by him to reconcile all things unto himself; by him, I say, whether they be things in earth, or things in heaven. 21 And you, that were sometime alienated and enemies in your mind by wicked works, yet now hath he reconciled 22 In the body of his flesh through death, to present you holy and unblameable and unreproveable in his sight:

Colossians 2:9 For in him dwelleth all the fulness of the Godhead bodily. 10 And ye are complete in him, which is the head of all principality and power:

Phillipians 4:19 But my God shall supply all your need according to his riches in glory by Christ Jesus

Ephesians 2:4 But God, who is rich in mercy, for his great love wherewith he loved us, 5 Even when we were dead in sins, hath quickened us together with Christ, (by grace ye are saved;) 6 And hath raised us up together, and made us sit together in heavenly places in Christ Jesus: 7 That in the ages to come he might shew the exceeding riches of his grace in his kindness toward us through Christ Jesus. 8 For by grace are ye saved through faith; and that not of yourselves: it is the gift of God: 9 Not of works, lest any man should boast. 10 For we are his workmanship, created in Christ Jesus unto good works, which God hath before ordained that we should walk in them.

Jude v24 Now unto him that is able to keep you from falling, and to present you faultless before the presence of his glory with exceeding joy

2 Peter 1:4 And because of his glory and excellence, he has given us great and precious promises. These are the promises that enable you to share his divine nature and escape the world's corruption caused by human desires.
Jeremiah 29:11 For I know the plans I have for you," says the Lord. "They are plans for good and not for disaster, to give you a future and a hope.

Matthew 11:28-29 "Come to me, all you who are weary and burdened, and I will give you rest. Take my yoke upon you and learn from me, for I am gentle and humble in heart, and you will find rest for your souls.

Proverbs 1:33 But all who listen to me will live in peace, untroubled by fear of harm."

Isaiah 40:29-31 He gives power to the weak and strength to the powerless. Even youths will become weak and tired, and young men will fall in exhaustion. But those who trust in the Lord will find new strength. They will soar high on wings like eagles. They will run and not grow weary. They will walk and not faint.

Romans 8:37-39 No, despite all these things, overwhelming victory is ours through Christ, who loved us. And I am convinced that nothing can ever separate us from God's love. Neither death nor life, neither angels nor demons, neither our fears for today nor our worries about tomorrow—not even the powers of hell can separate us from God's love. No power in the sky above or in the earth below—indeed, nothing in all creation will ever be able to separate us from the love of God that is revealed in Christ Jesus our Lord.

John 14:27 "I am leaving you with a gift—peace of mind and heart. And the peace I give is a gift the world cannot give. So don't be troubled or afraid.

Romans 10:9 If you confess with your mouth that Jesus is Lord and believe in your heart that God raised him from the dead, you will be saved.

Romans 6:23 For the wages of sin is death, but the free gift of God is eternal life through Christ Jesus our Lord. The promises of God are powerful and awesome to grasp. I pray that these scriptures about God's promises were helpful to you today.

1 Corinthians 10:13 There hath no temptation taken you but such as is common to man: but God is faithful, who will not suffer you to be tempted above that ye are able; but will with the temptation also make a way to escape, that ye may be able to bear it.

Exodus 15:26 And said, If thou wilt diligently hearken to the voice of the LORD thy God, and wilt do that which is right in his sight, and wilt give ear to his commandments, and keep all his statutes, I will put none of these diseases upon thee, which I have brought upon the Egyptians: for I am the LORD that healeth thee.

IDENTITY PROMISES

**No matter how many promises are made,
they are yes and amen in Christ**

Establishing your heart in your new identity in Christ is necessary
for living in God's promises. You are transformed by the renewing
of your mind, specifically to the truth of who you are in Him.
Writing the truth of God on the tablet of your heart will empower
you to see dramatic changes in your daily life. Don't just read these
passages, try to FEEL them as well. You do what you feel, what if
you could change how you naturally feel about God's promises?

Meditate until you experience the emotions associated with these
promises. As you read through each passage, pause a moment on
each one and ask yourself if you feel each one is true about you.

The truth is, because you are in Christ, each and everyone is true
of you. If you can feel righteous or holy or powerful over sin, you
heart will be open to God's grace to experience victory over sin in
your life.

If you feel it, you can believe it. If you can believe it you can
experience. Your victory over sin, depression, lack, anger or any
other struggle will manifest as your heart becomes persuaded of
the truth of your new identity in Christ.

I am complete in Him Who is the Head of all principality and power (Colossians 2:10).

I am alive with Christ (Ephesians 2:5).

I am free from the law of sin and death (Romans 8:2).

I am far from oppression, and fear does not come near me (Isaiah 54:14).

I am born of God, and the evil one does not touch me (1 John 5:18).

I am holy and without blame before Him in love (Ephesians 1:4; 1 Peter 1:16).

I have the mind of Christ (1 Corinthians 2:16; Philippians 2:5).

I have the peace of God that passes all understanding (Philippians 4:7).

I have the Greater One living in me; greater is He Who is in me than he who is in the world (1 John 4:4).

I have received the gift of righteousness and reign as a king in life by Jesus Christ (Romans 5:17).

I have received the spirit of wisdom and revelation in the knowledge of Jesus, the eyes of my understanding being enlightened (Ephesians 1:17-18).

I have received the power of the Holy Spirit to lay hands on the sick and see them recover, to cast out demons, to speak with new tongues. I have power over all the power of the enemy, and nothing shall by any means harm me (Mark 16:17-18; Luke 10:17-19).

I have put off the old man and have put on the new man, which is renewed in the knowledge after the image of Him Who created me (Colossians 3:9-10).

I have given, and it is given to me; good measure, pressed down, shaken together, and running over, men give into my bosom (Luke 6:38).

I have no lack for my God supplies all of my need according to His riches in glory by Christ Jesus
(Philippians 4:19).

I can quench all the fiery darts of the wicked one with my shield of faith (Ephesians 6:16).

I can do all things through Christ Jesus (Philippians 4:13).

I show forth the praises of God Who has called me out of darkness into His marvelous light (1 Peter 2:9).

I am God's child for I am born again of the incorruptible seed of the Word of God, which lives and abides forever (1 Peter 1:23).

I am God's workmanship, created in Christ unto good works (Ephesians 2:10).

I am a new creature in Christ (2 Corinthians 5:17).

I am a spirit being alive to God
(Romans 6:11;1 Thessalonians 5:23).

I am a believer, and the light of the Gospel shines in my mind (2 Corinthians 4:4).

I am a doer of the Word and blessed in my actions (James 1:22,25).

I am a joint-heir with Christ (Romans 8:17).

I am more than a conqueror through Him Who loves me (Romans 8:37).

I am an overcomer by the blood of the Lamb and the word of my testimony (Revelation 12:11).

I am a partaker of His divine nature (2 Peter 1:3-4).

I am an ambassador for Christ (2 Corinthians 5:20).

I am part of a chosen generation, a royal priesthood, a holy nation, a purchased people (1 Peter 2:9).

I am the righteousness of God in Jesus Christ (2 Corinthians 5:21).

I am the temple of the Holy Spirit; I am not my own (1 Corinthians 6:19).

I am the head and not the tail; I am above only and not beneath (Deuteronomy 28:13).

I am the light of the world (Matthew 5:14).

I am His elect, full of mercy, kindness, humility, and long-suffering (Romans 8:33; Colossians 3:12).

I am forgiven of all my sins and washed in the Blood (Ephesians 1:7).

I am delivered from the power of darkness and translated into God's kingdom (Colossians 1:13).

I am redeemed from the curse of sin, sickness, and poverty (Deuteronomy 28:15-68; Galatians 3:13).

I am firmly rooted, built up, established in my faith and overflowing with gratitude (Colossians 2:7).

I am called of God to be the voice of His praise (Psalm 66:8; 2 Timothy 1:9).

I am healed by the stripes of Jesus (Isaiah 53:5; 1 Peter 2:24).

I am raised up with Christ and seated in heavenly places (Ephesians 2:6; Colossians 2:12).

I am greatly loved by God (Romans 1:7; Ephesians 2:4; Colossians 3:12; 1 Thessalonians 1:4).

I am strengthened with all might according to His glorious power (Colossians 1:11).

I am submitted to God, and the devil flees from me because I resist him in the Name of Jesus (James 4:7).

I press on toward the goal to win the prize to which God in Christ Jesus is calling us upward (Philippians 3:14).

For God has not given us a spirit of fear; but of power, love, and a sound mind (2 Timothy 1:7).

It is not I who live, but Christ lives in me (Galatians 2:20).

PROMISES FROM THE NEW TESTAMENT

**No matter how many promises are made,
they are yes and amen in Christ**

MATTHEW

6:6 "But you, when you pray, go into your inner room, close your door and pray to your Father who is in secret, and **your Father who sees what is done in secret will reward you.**

6:25 "For this reason I say to you, **do not be worried about your life, as to what you will eat or what you will drink; nor for your body, as to what you will put on.** Is not life more than food, and the body more than clothing? 26 "Look at the birds of the air, that they do not sow, nor reap nor gather into barns, and yet your heavenly Father feeds them. **Are you not worth much more than they?** 27 "And who of you by being worried can add a single hour to his life? 28 "And why are you worried about clothing? Observe how the lilies of the field grow; they do not toil nor do they spin, 29 yet I say to you that not even Solomon in all his glory clothed himself like one of these.

30 "But if God so clothes the grass of the field, which is alive today and tomorrow is thrown into the furnace, will He not much more clothe you? You of little faith!

31 "Do not worry then, saying, 'What will we eat?' or 'What will we drink?' or 'What will we wear for clothing?' 32 "For the Gentiles eagerly seek all these things; for your heavenly Father knows that you need all these things. 33 "**But seek first His kingdom and His righteousness, and all these things will be added to you.** 34 "So do not worry about tomorrow; for tomorrow will care for itself. Each day has enough trouble of its own.

7:7 "**Ask, and it will be given to you; seek, and you will find; knock, and it will be opened to you. 8 "For everyone who asks receives, and he who seeks finds, and to him who knocks it will be opened.** 9 "Or what man is there among you who, when his son asks for a loaf, will give him a stone? 10 "Or if he asks for a fish, he will not give him a snake, will he? 11 "If you then, being evil, know how to give good gifts to your children, **how much more will your Father who is in heaven give what is good to those who ask Him**!

9:6 "But so that you may know that the Son of Man has authority on earth to forgive sins"—then He said to the paralytic, "**Get up, pick up your bed and go home.**" 7 And he got up and went home.

9:35 Jesus was going through all the cities and villages, teaching in their synagogues and proclaiming the gospel of the kingdom, and healing every kind of disease and every kind of sickness.

10:1 Jesus summoned His twelve disciples and **gave them authority over unclean spirits, to cast them out, and to heal every kind of disease and every kind of sickness.**

11:28 "Come to Me, all who are weary and heavy-laden, and I will give you rest. 29 "Take My yoke upon you and learn from Me, for I am gentle and humble in heart, and YOU WILL FIND REST FOR YOUR SOULS. 30 "For My yoke is easy and My burden is light."

12:40 for just as JONAH WAS THREE DAYS AND THREE NIGHTS IN THE BELLY OF THE SEA MONSTER, so will the Son of Man be three days and three nights in the heart of the earth.

13:41 "The Son of Man will send forth His angels, and they will gather out of His kingdom all stumbling blocks, and those who commit lawlessness, 42 and will throw them into the furnace of fire; in that place there will be weeping and gnashing of teeth. 43 "Then **THE RIGHTEOUS WILL SHINE FORTH AS THE SUN in the kingdom of their Father**. He who has ears, let him hear.

16:19 **"I will give you the keys of the kingdom of heaven; and whatever you bind on earth shall have been bound in heaven, and whatever you loose on earth shall have been loosed in heaven**."

25:34 "Then the King will say to those on His right, 'Come, you who are blessed of My Father, **inherit the kingdom prepared for you from the foundation of the world**. 35 'For I was hungry, and you gave Me something to eat; I was thirsty, and you gave Me something to drink; I was a stranger, and you invited Me in; 36 naked, and you clothed Me; I was sick, and you visited Me; I was in prison, and you came to Me.'

26:26 While they were eating, Jesus took some bread, and after a blessing, He broke it and gave it to the disciples, and said, "Take, eat; this is My body." 27And when He had taken a cup and given thanks, He gave it to them, saying, "Drink from it, all of you; 28 for **this is My blood of the covenant, which is poured out for many for forgiveness of sins**.

28:5 The angel said to the women, **"Do not be afraid**; for I know that you are looking for Jesus who has been crucified. 6 "He is not here, for He has risen, just as He said. Come, see the place where He was lying.

MARK

1:17 And Jesus said to them, "Follow Me, and I will make you become fishers of men."

1:34 And He healed many who were ill with various diseases, and cast out many demons; and **He was not permitting the demons to speak, because they knew who He was.**

1:41 Moved with compassion, Jesus stretched out His hand and touched him, and said to him, **"I am willing; be cleansed."**

JESUS IS WILLING TO HEAL YOU

2:10 "But so that you may know that the Son of Man has authority on earth to forgive sins"—He said to the paralytic, 11 "I say to you, **get up, pick up your pallet and go home."** 12 And he got up and immediately picked up the pallet and went out in the sight of everyone, so that they were all amazed and were glorifying God, saying, "We have never seen anything like this."

2:17 And hearing this, Jesus said to them, "It is not those who are healthy who need a physician, but those who are sick; I did not come to call the righteous, but sinners."

3:11 Whenever the unclean spirits saw Him, they would fall down before Him and shout, "You are the Son of God!"

3:14 And He appointed twelve, so that they would be with Him and that He could send them out to preach, 15 and to have authority to cast out the demons.

5:36 But Jesus, overhearing what was being spoken, said to the synagogue official, **"Do not be afraid any longer, only believe."**

6:12 They went out and preached that men should repent. 13 **And they were casting out many demons and were anointing with oil many sick people and healing them.**

8:31 He then began to teach them that the Son of Man must suffer many things and be rejected by the elders, the chief priests and the teachers of the law, and that **he must be killed and after three days rise again**.

9:31because he was teaching his disciples. He said to them, "The Son of Man is going to be delivered into the hands of men. They will kill him, **and after three days he will rise**."

10:26 The disciples were even more amazed, and said to each other, "Who then can be saved?" 27 Jesus looked at them and said, "**With man this is impossible, but not with God; all things are possible with God**."

11:22 "Have faith in God," Jesus answered. 23 "Truly I tell you, if anyone says to this mountain, 'Go, throw yourself into the sea,' and does not doubt in their heart but believes that what they say will happen, it will be done for them. 24 Therefore I tell you, **whatever you ask for in prayer, believe that you have received it, and it will be yours**.

14:24 "This is my blood of the covenant, which is poured out for many," he said to them.

14:62 "I am," said Jesus. "And you will see the Son of Man sitting at the right hand of the Mighty One and coming on the clouds of heaven."

16:15 He said to them, "Go into all the world and preach the gospel to all creation. 16 Whoever believes and is baptized will be saved, but whoever does not believe will be condemned. 17 And these signs will accompany those who believe: In my name they will drive out demons; they will speak in new tongues; 18 they will pick up snakes with their hands; and when they drink deadly poison, it will not hurt them at all; they will place their hands on sick people, and they will get well."

LUKE

1:32 He will be great and will be called the Son of the Most High. The Lord God will give him the throne of his father David, 33 and he will reign over Jacob's descendants forever; his kingdom will never end."

2:14 Glory to God in the highest, and on earth peace, good will toward men.

3:5 Every valley shall be filled, and every mountain and hill shall be brought low; and the crooked shall be made straight, and the rough ways shall be made smooth; 6 And all flesh shall see the salvation of God.

JOHN

1:12-13 **But as many as received him, to them gave he power to become the children of God,** even to them that believe on his name: Who were born, not of blood, nor of the will of the flesh, nor of the will of man, but of God.

3:16 For God so loved the world, that he gave his only begotten Son, that whosoever believes in him should not perish, but have everlasting life. 17 For God sent not his Son into the world to condemn the world; but that the world through him might be saved. 18 He that believes on him is not condemned: but he that believes not is condemned already, because he has not believed in the name of the only begotten Son of God.

5:24 Verily, verily, I say unto you, **He that hears my word, and believes on him that sent me, has everlasting life, and shall not come into condemnation; but is passed from death unto life.**

10:9 **I am the door: by me if any man enter in, he shall be saved,** and shall go in and out, and find pasture. 10 The thief comes not, but to steal, and to kill, and to destroy: **I am come that they might have life, and that they might have it more**

abundantly.

11:25 Jesus said unto her, **I am the resurrection, and the life: he that believes in me, though he were dead, yet shall he live**: 26 And whosoever lives and believes in me shall never die. Do you believe this?

12:26 If any man serves me, let him follow me; and **where I am, there shall also my servant be**: if any man serves me, him will my Father honor.

12:31 Now is the judgment of this world: now shall the prince of this world be cast out. 32 And I, if I be lifted up from the earth, will draw all (judgment) unto me.

12:46 I am come a light into the world, that **whosoever believes on me should not abide in darkness**. 47 And if any man hear my words, and believe not, I judge him not: for **I came not to judge the world, but to save the world**.

14:1 Let not your heart be troubled: you believe in God, believe also in me.

2 In my Father's house are many mansions: if it were not so, I would have told you. **I go to prepare a place for you. 3 And if I go and prepare a place for you, I will come again, and receive you unto myself; that where I am, there you may be also.**

14:12 Verily, verily, I say unto you, **He that believes on me, the works that I do shall he do also; and greater works than these shall he do; because I go unto my Father. 13 And whatsoever you shall ask in my name, that will I do, that the Father may be glorified in the Son. 14 If you shall ask anything in my name, I will do it.**

14:18 I will not leave you comfortless: I will come to you.

14:26 But the Comforter, who is the Holy Spirit, whom the Father will send in my name, **he shall teach you all things, and bring all things to your remembrance, whatsoever I have said unto you.** 27 **Peace I leave with you, my peace I give unto you: not as the world gives, give I unto you. Let not your heart be troubled, neither let it be afraid.**

15:4 Abide in me, and I in you. As the branch cannot bear fruit of itself, except it abide in the vine; no more can you, except you abide in me. 5 I am the vine, you are the branches: **He that abides in me, and I in him, the same brings forth much fruit**: for without me you can do nothing.

15:7 If you abide in me, and my words abide in you, you shall ask what you will, and it shall be done unto you.

15:11 These things have I spoken unto you, that my joy might remain in you, and that your joy might be full.

15:15 From now on I call you not servants; for the servant knows not what his lord does: but **I have called you friends**; for all things that I have heard of my Father I have made known unto you.

15:26 But when the Comforter is come, whom **I will send unto you from the Father, even the Spirit of truth**, who proceeds from the Father, he shall testify of me: 27 And you also shall bear witness, because you have been with me from the beginning.

16:13 But when he, the Spirit of truth, is come, he will guide you into all truth: for he shall not speak of himself; but whatsoever he shall hear, that shall he speak: and he will show you things to come.

16:23 And in that day you shall ask me nothing. Verily, verily, I say unto you, **whatsoever you shall ask the Father in my name, he will give it to you.**

16:27 For the Father himself loves you, because you have loved me, and have believed that I came out from God.

16:33 These things I have spoken unto you, that **in me you might have peace**. In the world you shall have tribulation: but be of good cheer; I have overcome the world.

17:3 And this is life eternal, that they might know you the only true God, and Jesus Christ, whom you have sent.

17:20 Neither pray I for these alone, but for them also who shall believe on me through their word; 21 **That they all may be one; as you, Father, are in me, and I in you, that they also may be one in us: that the world may believe that you have sent me.** 22 And **the glory which you gave me I have given them; that they may be one, even as we are one**: 23 I in them, and you in me, that they may be made perfect in one; and that the world may know that you have sent me, and have loved them, as you have loved me. 24 Father, I will that they also, whom you have given me, be with me where I am; that they may behold my glory, which you have given me: for you loved me before the foundation of the world. 25 O righteous Father, the world has not known you: but I have known you, and these have known that you have sent me. 26 And I have declared unto them your name, and will declare it: **that the love with which you have loved me may be in them, and I in them.**

20:21 Then said Jesus to them again, **Peace be unto you: as my Father has sent me, even so send I you**. 22 And when he had said this, he breathed on them, and said unto them, **Receive you the Holy Spirit:**

20:29 Jesus said unto him, Thomas, because you have seen me, you have believed: blessed are they that have not seen, and yet have believed.

ACTS

1:5 For John truly baptized with water; but you shall be baptized with the Holy Spirit not many days from now.

1:8 But **you shall receive power, after the Holy Spirit has come upon you**: and you shall be witnesses unto me both in Jerusalem, and in all Judea, and in Samaria, and unto the uttermost part of the earth.

2:1 And when the day of Pentecost was fully come, they were all with one accord in one place. 2 And suddenly there came a sound from heaven as of a rushing mighty wind, and it filled all the house where they were sitting. 3 And there appeared unto them separated tongues like as of fire, and it sat upon each of them. 4 **And they were all filled with the Holy Spirit, and began to speak with other tongues, as the Spirit gave them utterance.**

2:21 And it shall come to pass, that whosoever shall call on the name of the Lord shall be saved.

2:38 Then Peter said unto them, Repent, and **be baptized every one of you in the name of Jesus Christ for the remission of sins, and you shall receive the gift of the Holy Spirit.** 39 For the promise is unto you, and to your children, and to all that are afar off, even as many as the Lord our God shall call.

3:6 Then Peter said, Silver and gold have I none; but such as I have I give you: In the name of Jesus Christ of Nazareth rise up and walk.

3:19 Repent therefore, and be converted, that your sins may be blotted out, when the times of refreshing shall come from the presence of the Lord

3:25 **You are the children of the prophets, and of the covenant** which God made with our fathers, saying unto Abraham, And in your descendants shall all the families of the earth be blessed.

4:12 **Neither is there salvation in any other: for there is no other name under heaven given among men, by which we must be saved.**

4:33 And with great power gave the apostles witness of the resurrection of the Lord Jesus: and great grace was upon them all.

10:40 **Him God raised up the third day, and showed him openly**; 41 Not to all the people, but unto witnesses chosen before of God, even to us, who did eat and drink with him after he rose from the dead. 42 And he commanded us to preach unto the people, and to testify that it is he who was ordained of God to be the Judge of the living and dead. 43 **To him give all the prophets witness, that through his name whosoever believes in him shall receive remission of sins**.

11:16 Then remembered I the word of the Lord, how he said, John indeed baptized with water; **but you shall be baptized with the Holy Spirit**.

13:32 And we declare unto you glad tidings, **how the promise which was made unto the fathers**, 33 God has fulfilled the same unto us their children, in that he has raised up Jesus again; as it is also written in the second psalm, You are my Son, this day have I begotten you. 34 And as concerning that he raised him up from the dead, now no more to return to corruption, he said in this way, I will give you the sure mercies of David. 35 Therefore he says also in another psalm, You shall not allow your Holy One to see corruption. 36 For David, after he had served his own generation by the will of God, fell asleep, and was laid with his fathers, and saw corruption: 37 But he, whom God raised again, saw no corruption. 38 Be it known unto you therefore, men and brethren, that through this man is preached unto you the forgiveness of sins: 39 And by him all that believe are justified from all things, from which you could not be justified by the law of Moses.

16:31 And they said, Believe on the Lord Jesus Christ, and you shall be saved, and your house.

17:27 That they should seek the Lord, if perhaps they might feel after him, and find him, though he be not far from every one of us: 28 For in him we live, and move, and have our being; as certain also of your own poets have said, For we are also his offspring.

18:9 Then spoke the Lord to Paul in the night by a vision, Be not afraid, but speak, and hold not your peace: 10 For I am with you, and no man shall set on you to hurt you: for I have many people in this city.

ROMANS

1:16 For I am not ashamed of the gospel of Christ: for **it is the power of God unto salvation to every one that believes**; to the Jew first, and also to the Greek. 17 For **in it is the righteousness of God revealed from faith to faith**: as it is written, The just shall live by faith.

3:21 But now the righteousness of God apart from the law is manifested, being witnessed by the law and the prophets;

22 Even the righteousness of God which is by faith in Jesus Christ unto all and upon all them that believe: for there is no difference: 23 For all have sinned, and come short of the glory of God; 24 **Being justified freely by his grace through the redemption that is in Christ Jesus: 25 Whom God has set forth to be a propitiation through faith in his blood, to declare his righteousness for the remission of sins that are past, through the forbearance of God;** 26 To declare, I say, at this time his righteousness: that he might be just, and **the justifier of him who believes in Jesus**. 27 Where is boasting then? It is excluded. By what law? of works? Nay: but by the law of faith. 28 Therefore we conclude that **a man is justified by faith without the deeds of the law.**

5:1 Therefore being justified by faith, we have peace with God through our Lord Jesus Christ: 2 By whom also we have access by faith into this grace in which we stand, and rejoice in hope of the glory of God.

5:5 And hope makes not ashamed; because **the love of God is shed abroad in our hearts by the Holy Spirit** who is given unto us

5:8 But God commends his love toward us, in that, while we were yet sinners, Christ died for us.

9 **Much more then, being now justified by his blood, we shall be saved from wrath through him.** 10 For if, when we were enemies, we were reconciled to God by the death of his Son, much more, being reconciled, **we shall be saved by his life**. 11 And not only so, but we also rejoice in God through our Lord Jesus Christ, by whom we have now received the reconciliation.

6:5 For if we have been united with him in the likeness of his death, **we shall be also in the likeness of his resurrection**: 6 Knowing this, that **our old man is crucified with him, that the body of sin might be destroyed, that we should no longer serve sin**. 7 For he that is dead is freed from sin. 8 Now if we are dead with Christ, **we believe that we shall also live with him**: 9 Knowing that Christ being raised from the dead dies no more; death has no more dominion over him. 10 For in that he died, he died unto sin once: but in that he lives, he lives unto God.

6:11 Likewise reckon you also yourselves to be dead indeed unto sin, but alive unto God through Jesus Christ our Lord.

6:14 For sin shall not have dominion over you: for you are not under the law, but under grace.

6:17 But God be thanked, that you were the servants of sin, but you have obeyed from the heart that form of doctrine which was delivered you. 18 **Being then made free from sin, you became the servants of righteousness.**

6:22 But now being made free from sin, and become servants to God, you have your fruit unto holiness, and the end everlasting life. 23 For the wages of sin is death; but **the gift of God is eternal life through Jesus Christ our Lord.**

7:4 Therefore, my brethren, **you also have become dead to the law by the body of Christ;** that you should be married to another, even to him who is raised from the dead, that we should bring forth fruit unto God. 5 For when we were in the flesh, the passions of sins, which were by the law, did work in our members to bring forth fruit unto death. 6 **But now we are delivered from the law, being dead to that in which we were held; that we should serve in newness of spirit, and not in the oldness of the letter.**

8:1 **There is therefore now no condemnation to them who are in Christ Jesus. 2 For the law of the Spirit of life in Christ Jesus has made me free from the law of sin and death.** 3 For what the law could not do, in that it was weak through the flesh, God sending his own Son in the likeness of sinful flesh, and for sin, condemned sin in the flesh: 4 That the righteousness of the law might be fulfilled in us, who walk not after the flesh, but after the Spirit.

8:9 **But you are not in the flesh, but in the Spirit, if so be that the Spirit of God dwells in you.** Now if any man have not the Spirit of Christ, he is none of his. 10 And **if Christ be in you, the body is dead because of sin; but the Spirit is life because of**

righteousness. 11 But if the Spirit of him that raised up Jesus from the dead dwells in you, **he that raised up Christ from the dead shall also bring to life your mortal bodies by his Spirit that dwells in you.**

8:14 For as many as are led by the Spirit of God, they are the sons of God. 15 **For you have not received the spirit of bondage again to fear; but you have received the Spirit of adoption**, by which we cry, Abba, Father. 16 The Spirit himself bears witness with our spirit, that we are the children of God: 17 And if children, then heirs; heirs of God, and joint-heirs with Christ; if so be that we suffer with him, so that we may be also glorified together.

10:4 For Christ is the end of the law for righteousness to everyone that believes.

10:9 That **if you shall confess with your mouth the Lord Jesus, and shall believe in your heart that God has raised him from the dead, you shall be saved.** 10 For with the heart man believes unto righteousness; and with the mouth confession is made unto salvation. 11 For the scripture says, **Whosoever believes on him shall not be ashamed.** 12 For there is no difference between the Jew and the Greek: for the same Lord over all is rich unto all that call upon him. 13 For whosoever shall call upon the name of the Lord shall be saved.

12:2 And be not conformed to this world: but be transformed by the renewing of your mind, that you may prove what is that good, and acceptable, and perfect, will of God.

14:17 For the kingdom of God is not food and drink; but righteousness, and peace, and joy in the Holy Spirit.

15:13 Now the God of hope fill you with all joy and peace in believing, that you may abound in hope, through the power of the Holy Spirit.

I CORINTHIANS

1:4 I thank my God always on your behalf, for the grace of God which is given you by Jesus Christ; 5 That **in every thing you are enriched by him**, in all utterance, and in all knowledge; 6 Even as the testimony of Christ was confirmed in you: 7 So that **you come behind in no gift**; waiting for the coming of our Lord Jesus Christ: 8 Who shall also confirm you unto the end, that **you may be blameless in the day of our Lord Jesus Christ.** 9 **God is faithful**, by whom you were called unto the fellowship of his Son Jesus Christ our Lord.

1:30 And of him are you in Christ Jesus, who of God is made unto us wisdom, and righteousness, and sanctification, and redemption:

2:9 But as it is written, Eye has not seen, nor ear heard, neither have entered into the heart of man, the things which God has prepared for them that love him. 10 **But God has revealed them unto us by his Spirit**: for the Spirit searches all things, yea, the deep things of God.

2:12 Now we have received, not the spirit of the world, but the Spirit who is of God; **that we might know the things that are freely given to us of God.**

2:16 For who has known the mind of the Lord, that he may instruct him? **But we have the mind of Christ.**

3:16 Know you not that you are the temple of God, and that **the Spirit of God dwells in you?**

3:23 And you are Christ's; and Christ is God's.

6:11 And such were some of you: but you are washed, but **you are sanctified**, but **you are justified in the name of the Lord Jesus**, and by the Spirit of our God.

6:17 But he that is joined unto the Lord is one spirit.

6:19 What? know you not that **your body is the temple of the Holy Spirit who is in you,** whom you have of God, and you are not your own? 20 For you are bought with a price: therefore glorify God in your body, and in your spirit, which are God's.

10:13 There has no temptation taken you but such as is common to man: but God is faithful, who will not allow you to be tempted above that you are able; but will with the temptation also **make a way to escape,** that you may be able to bear it.

15:20 But **now is Christ risen from the dead,** and become the firstfruits of them that slept. 21 For since by man came death, by man came also the resurrection of the dead. 22 For as in Adam all die, even so in Christ shall all be made alive. 23 But every man in his own order: Christ the firstfruits; afterward they that are Christ's at his coming.

15:48 As is the earthy, such are they also that are earthy: and as is the heavenly, such are they also that are heavenly. 49 And as we have borne the image of the earthy, **we shall also bear the image of the heavenly.**

15:52 In a moment, in the twinkling of an eye, at the last trump: for the trumpet shall sound, and the dead shall be raised incorruptible, and **we shall be changed.** 53 **For this corruptible must put on incorruption, and this mortal must put on immortality.** 54 So when this corruptible shall have put on incorruption, and this mortal shall have put on immortality, then shall be brought to pass the saying that is written, Death is swallowed up in victory.

15:58 Therefore, my beloved brethren, be steadfast, unmovable, always abounding in the work of the Lord, since **you know that your labor is not in vain in the Lord.**

II CORINTHIANS

1:3 Blessed be God, even the Father of our Lord Jesus Christ, the Father of mercies, and the God of all comfort; 4 **Who comforts us in all our tribulation**, that we may be able to comfort them who are in any trouble, by the comfort with which we ourselves are comforted of God.

1:20 **For all the promises of God in him are yea, and in him Amen, unto the glory of God by us.** 21 Now he who establishes us with you in Christ, and has anointed us, is God; 22 Who has also sealed us, and **given the earnest of the Spirit in our hearts.**

2:14 Now thanks be unto God, **who always causes us to triumph** in Christ, and makes manifest the fragrance of his knowledge by us in every place.

3:18 But we all, with unveiled face beholding as in a mirror the glory of the Lord, **are changed into the same image** from glory to glory, even as by the Spirit of the Lord.

4:5 For we preach not ourselves, but Christ Jesus the Lord; and ourselves your servants for Jesus' sake. 6 For God, who commanded the light to shine out of darkness, has shined in our hearts, **to give the light of the knowledge of the glory of God in the face of Jesus Christ.** 7 But we have this treasure in earthen vessels, that the excellency of the power may be of God, and not of us.

4:18 While we look not at the things which are seen, but at the things which are not seen: for the things which are seen are temporal; **but the things which are not seen are eternal.**

5:1 For we know that if our earthly house of this tabernacle were dissolved, **we have a building of God**, a house not made with hands, **eternal in the heavens.**

5:5 Now he that has made us for the same thing is God, who also has given unto us the earnest of the Spirit. 6 Therefore we are always confident, knowing that, while we are at home in the body, we are absent from the Lord:

5:17 Therefore if any man be in Christ, **he is a new creation**: old things are passed away; behold, all things are become new. 18 And all things are of God, **who has reconciled us to himself** by Jesus Christ, and has given to us the ministry of reconciliation; 19 That is, that God was in Christ, reconciling the world unto himself, **not imputing their trespasses unto them**; and has committed unto us the word of reconciliation. 20 Now then **we are ambassadors for Christ**, as though God did beseech you by us: we pray you on Christ's behalf, be reconciled to God. 21 **For he has made him, who knew no sin, to be sin for us; that we might be made the righteousness of God in him.**

6:16 And what agreement has the temple of God with idols? **for you are the temple of the living God**; as God has said, I will dwell in them, and walk in them; and **I will be their God, and they shall be my people**.

9:6 But this I say, He who sows sparingly shall reap also sparingly; and **he who sows bountifully shall reap also bountifully**. 7 Every man according as he purposes in his heart, so let him give; not grudgingly, or of necessity: for **God loves a cheerful giver**. 8 **And God is able to make all grace abound toward you; that you, always having all sufficiency in all things, may abound to every good work:**

12:9 And he said unto me, **My grace is sufficient for you**: for my strength is made perfect in weakness. Most gladly therefore will I rather boast in my weaknesses, that the power of Christ may rest upon me.

GALATIANS

1:3 Grace be to you and peace from God the Father, and from our Lord Jesus Christ, 4 Who **gave himself for our sins, that he might deliver us from this present evil world**, according to the will of God our Father:

2:16 Knowing that a man is not justified by the works of the law, **but by the faith of Jesus Christ**, even we have believed in Jesus Christ, that **we might be justified by the faith of Christ, and not by the works of the law**: for by the works of the law shall no flesh be justified.

2:19 For I through the law am dead to the law, that I might live unto God. 20 I am crucified with Christ: nevertheless I live; yet not I, but **Christ lives in me**: and the life which I now live in the flesh **I live by the faith of the Son of God**, who loved me, and gave himself for me. 21 I do not nullify the grace of God: for if righteousness comes by the law, then Christ is dead in vain.

3:11 But that no man is justified by the law in the sight of God, it is evident: for, **The just shall live by faith.**

3:13 **Christ has redeemed us from the curse of the law**, being made a curse for us: for it is written, Cursed is every one that hangs on a tree: 14 That the blessing of Abraham might come on the Gentiles through Jesus Christ; that **we might receive the promise of the Spirit through faith**.

3:18 For if the inheritance is of the law, it is no more of promise: but **God gave it to Abraham by promise**.

3:24 Therefore the law was our schoolmaster to bring us unto Christ, **that we might be justified by faith.**

3:26 For **you are all the children of God by faith in Christ Jesus**. 27 For as many of you as have been baptized into Christ have put on Christ. 28 There is neither Jew nor Greek, there is neither bond nor free, there is neither male nor female: for you are all one in Christ Jesus. 29 And **if you are Christ's, then are you**

Abraham's descendants, and heirs according to the promise.

4:4 But when the fullness of the time came, God sent forth his Son, made of a woman, made under the law, 5 To **redeem them that were under the law, that we might receive the adoption as sons.** 6 And because you are sons, God has sent forth the Spirit of his Son into your hearts, crying, Abba, Father. 7 Therefore **you are no more a servant, but a son**; and if a son, then an heir of God through Christ.

5:5 For we through the Spirit wait for the hope of righteousness by faith. 6 For in Jesus Christ neither circumcision avails anything, nor uncircumcision; but **faith which works by love.**

5:16 This I say then, Walk in the Spirit, and **you shall not fulfill the lust of the flesh.**

6:8 For he that sows to his flesh shall of the flesh reap corruption; but **he that sows to the Spirit shall of the Spirit reap life everlasting.**

EPHESIANS

1:3 Blessed be the God and Father of our Lord Jesus Christ, **who has blessed us with all spiritual blessings in heavenly places in Christ**:

1:7 In whom we have redemption through his blood, the forgiveness of sins, according to the riches of his grace;

1:10 That in the dispensation of the fullness of times he might gather together in one all things in Christ, both which are in heaven, and which are on earth; even in him: 11 **In whom also we have obtained an inheritance,** being predestinated according to the purpose of him who works all things after the counsel of his own will: 12 **That we should be to the praise of his glory,** who first trusted in Christ.

1:17 That the God of our Lord Jesus Christ, the Father of glory, **may give unto you the spirit of wisdom and revelation in the knowledge of him**: 18 The eyes of **your understanding being enlightened**; that **you may know what is the hope of his calling**, and what is **the riches of the glory of his inheritance in the saints**, 19 And what is the exceeding greatness of his power toward us who believe, according to the working of his mighty power,

2:1 And you has he made alive, who were dead in trespasses and sins:

2:4 But God, who is rich in mercy, for **his great love with which he loved us, 5 Even when we were dead in sins, has made us alive together with Christ,** (by grace you are saved;) 6 And **has raised us up together, and made us sit together in heavenly places in Christ Jesus**: 7 That **in the ages to come he might show the exceeding riches of his grace in his kindness toward us through Christ Jesus.**

2:8 For by grace are you saved through faith; and that not of yourselves: it is the gift of God: 9 Not of works, lest any man should boast. 10 For we are his workmanship, created in Christ

Jesus unto good works, which God has before ordained that we should walk in them.

2:13 But now in Christ Jesus you who once were far off are made near by the blood of Christ. 14 For he is our peace, who has made both one, and has broken down the middle wall of partition between us; 15 Having abolished in his flesh the enmity, even the law of commandments contained in ordinances; to make in himself of two one new man, so making peace; 16 And that he might reconcile both unto God in one body by the cross, having slain the enmity thereby: 17 That Christ may dwell in your hearts by faith; that you, being rooted and grounded in love, 18 May be able to comprehend with all saints what is the breadth, and length, and depth, and height; 19 And to know the love of Christ, which passes knowledge, that you might be filled with all the fullness of God.

3:20 Now unto him that is able to do exceeding abundantly above all that we ask or think, according to the power that works in us,

4:23 And be renewed in the spirit of your mind; 24 And that you put on the new man, which after God is created in righteousness and true holiness.

5:8 For you were once darkness, but now are you light in the Lord: walk as children of light:

PHILIPPIANS

1:6 Being confident of this very thing, that **he who has begun a good work in you will complete it until the day of Jesus Christ**:

1:21 For to me to live is Christ, and to die is gain.

2:13 For it is God who works in you both to will and to do of his good pleasure.

3:7 But what things were gain to me, those I counted loss for Christ. 8 Yea doubtless, and **I count all things but loss for the excellency of the knowledge of Christ Jesus my Lord**: for whom I have suffered the loss of all things, and do count them but rubbish, that I may win Christ, 9 And be found in him, **not having my own righteousness, which is of the law, but that which is through the faith of Christ, the righteousness which is of God by faith**: 10 **That I may know him, and the power of his resurrection**, and the fellowship of his sufferings, being made conformable unto his death; 11 If by any means I might attain unto the resurrection of the dead.

3:20 For our citizenship is in heaven; from which also we look for the Savior, the Lord Jesus Christ: 21 Who shall change our humble body, that it may be fashioned like unto his glorious body, according to the working by which he is able even to subdue all things unto himself.

4:6 Be anxious for nothing; but in everything by prayer and supplication with thanksgiving let your requests be made known unto God. 7 And the peace of God, which passes all understanding, shall keep your hearts and minds through Christ Jesus.

4:13 I can do all things through Christ who strengthens me.

4:19 But my God shall supply all your need according to his riches in glory by Christ Jesus.

COLOSSIANS

1:12 Giving thanks unto the Father, **who has made us fit to be partakers of the inheritance of the saints in light**: 13 **Who has delivered us from the power of darkness, and has translated us into the kingdom of his dear Son**: 14 In whom we have redemption through his blood, even the forgiveness of sins:

1:20 And, **having made peace through the blood of his cross**, by him to reconcile all things unto himself; by him, I say, whether they be things in earth, or things in heaven. 21 And you, that were once alienated and enemies in your mind by wicked works, **yet now has he reconciled 22 In the body of his flesh through death, to present you holy and unblamable and unreprovable in his sight**:

1:27 **To whom God would make known what is the riches of the glory of this mystery among the Gentiles; which is Christ in you, the hope of glory:**

2:10 **And you are complete in him, who is the head of all principality and power:** 11 In whom also you are circumcised with the circumcision made without hands, in putting off the body of the sins of the flesh by the circumcision of Christ: 12 Buried with him in baptism, **in which also you are risen with him through the faith of the working of God**, who has raised him from the dead. 13 And you, being dead in your sins and the uncircumcision of your flesh, **has he made alive together with him**, having forgiven you all trespasses; 14 **Blotting out the handwriting of ordinances that was against us**, which was contrary to us, and took it out of the way, nailing it to his cross; 15 And having spoiled principalities and powers, he made a show of them openly, triumphing over them in it.

3:1 If you then be risen with Christ, seek those things which are above, where Christ sits on the right hand of God. 2 Set your affection on things above, not on things on the earth. 3 **For you are dead, and your life is hid with Christ in God. 4 When Christ, who is our life, shall appear, then shall you also appear with him in glory.**

I THESSALONIANS

1:10 And to wait for his Son from heaven, whom he raised from the dead, even Jesus, **who delivered us from the wrath to come**.

3:13 To the end **he may establish your hearts unblamable in holiness before God**, even our Father, at the coming of our Lord Jesus Christ with all his saints.

4:16 For the Lord himself shall descend from heaven with a shout, with the voice of the archangel, and with the trump of God: and the dead in Christ shall rise first: 17 Then we who are alive and remain shall be caught up together with them in the clouds, to meet the Lord in the air: and so shall we ever be with the Lord.

5:9 **For God has not appointed us to wrath, but to obtain salvation by our Lord Jesus Christ**, 10 Who died for us, that, whether we wake or sleep, we should live together with him.

5:23 And **the very God of peace sanctify you wholly**; and I pray God your whole spirit and soul and body be preserved blameless unto the coming of our Lord Jesus Christ.

II THESSALONIANS

1:10 When he shall come to be glorified in his saints, and **to be admired in all them that believe** (because our testimony among you was believed) in that day.

2:13 But we are bound to give thanks always to God for you, brethren **beloved of the Lord, because God has from the beginning chosen you to salvation through sanctification of the Spirit and belief of the truth**: 14 To which he called you by our gospel, to the obtaining of the glory of our Lord Jesus Christ.

2:16 Now our Lord Jesus Christ himself, and God, even our Father, **who has loved us**, and has given us everlasting encouragement and good hope through grace, 17 Encourage your hearts, and **establish you in every good word and work**.

3:3 But **the Lord is faithful, who shall establish you, and keep you from evil.** 4 And we have confidence in the Lord concerning you, that you both do and will do the things which we command you. 5 And **the Lord direct your hearts into the love of God, and into the patient waiting for Christ.**

3:16 Now the Lord of peace himself give you peace always by all means. The Lord be with you all.

I TIMOTHY

1:14 And the grace of our Lord was exceedingly abundant with faith and love which is in Christ Jesus. 15 This is a faithful saying, and worthy of all acceptance, that **Christ Jesus came into the world to save sinners;** of whom I am chief. 16 But for this cause I obtained mercy, that in me first Jesus Christ might show forth all longsuffering, for an example to them who should hereafter believe on him to life everlasting.

2:3 For this is good and acceptable in the sight of God our Savior; 4 **Who will have all men to be saved,** and to come unto the knowledge of the truth. 5 For there is one God, and **one mediator between God and men, the man Christ Jesus;** 6 Who gave himself a ransom for all, this to be a testimony at the proper time.

4:8 For bodily exercise profits for a little while: but godliness is profitable unto all things, having **promise of the life that now is, and of that which is to come.**

6:6 But godliness with contentment is great gain.

6:17 Charge them that are rich in this present age, that they be not haughty, nor trust in uncertain riches, but in **the living God, who gives us richly all things to enjoy;**

II TIMOTHY

1:7 For God has not given us the spirit of fear; but of **power, and of love, and of a sound mind**.

1:9 Who has saved us, and called us with a holy calling, not according to our works, but according to his own purpose and grace, which was given us in Christ Jesus before the world began 10 But is now made manifest by the appearing of our Savior Jesus Christ, who has abolished death, and has brought life and immortality to light through the gospel

1:12 For the which cause I also suffer these things: nevertheless I am not ashamed: for I know whom I have believed, and am persuaded that **he is able to keep that which I have committed unto him against that day**.

2:1 You therefore, my son, **be strong in the grace** that is in Christ Jesus.

2:11 It is a faithful saying: For if we be dead with him, **we shall also live with him**: 12 If we suffer, we shall also reign with him: if we deny him, he also will deny us: 13 If we believe not, yet **he abides faithful**: he cannot deny himself.

2:19 Nevertheless the foundation of God stands sure, having this seal, The Lord knows them that are his. And, Let every one that names the name of Christ depart from iniquity.

4:8 Henceforth there is laid up for me a crown of righteousness, which the Lord, the righteous judge, shall give me at that day: and not to me only, but unto all them also that love his appearing.

4:18 And **the Lord shall deliver me from every evil work**, and will preserve me unto his heavenly kingdom: to whom be glory forever and ever. Amen.

TITUS

2:11 For the grace of God that brings salvation has appeared to all men, 12 Teaching us that, denying ungodliness and worldly lusts, we should live sensibly, righteously, and godly, in this present world; 13 Looking for that blessed hope, and the glorious appearing of the great God and our Savior Jesus Christ; 14 Who gave himself for us, that he might redeem us from all iniquity, and purify unto himself a people for his own, zealous of good works.

3:4 But after the kindness and love of God our Savior toward man appeared, 5 Not by works of righteousness which we have done, but according to his mercy he saved us, by the washing of regeneration, and renewing of the Holy Spirit; 6 Whom he shed on us abundantly through Jesus Christ our Savior; 7 That being justified by his grace, we should be made heirs according to the hope of eternal life.

PHILEMON

6 That the sharing of your faith may become effective by the acknowledging of every good thing which is in you in Christ Jesus.

25 The grace of our Lord Jesus Christ be with your spirit. Amen.

HEBREWS

1:3 Who being the brightness of his glory, and the express image of his person, and upholding all things by the word of his power, when **he had by himself purged our sins**, sat down on the right hand of the Majesty on high

1:9 You have loved righteousness, and hated iniquity; therefore God, even your **God, has anointed you with the oil of gladness** above your fellows.

2:6 But one in a certain place testified, saying, What is man, that you are mindful of him? or the son of man, that you visit him? 7 **You made him a little lower than the angels; you crowned him with glory and honor, and did set him over the works of your hands: 8 You have put all things in subjection under his feet. For in that he put all in subjection under him**, he left nothing that is not put under him. But now we see not yet all things put under him. 9 But we see Jesus, who was made a little lower than the angels for the suffering of death, crowned with glory and honor; **that he by the grace of God should taste death for every man.**

2:18 For in that he himself has suffered being tempted, **he is able to help them that are tempted.**

3:14 For **we are made partakers of Christ**, if we hold the beginning of our confidence steadfast unto the end;

4:9 **There remains therefore a rest to the people of God.** 10 For **he that is entered into his rest, he also has ceased from his own works,** as God did from his. 11 **Let us labor therefore to enter into that rest,** lest any man fall after the same example of unbelief.

4:14 Seeing then that we have a great high priest, that is passed into the heavens, Jesus the Son of God, let us hold fast our profession.

15 For we have not a high priest who cannot be touched with the feeling of our weaknesses; but was in all points tempted like we are, yet without sin. 16 **Let us therefore come boldly unto the throne of grace, that we may obtain mercy, and find grace to help in time of need.**

6:17 So God, willing more abundantly to show unto the heirs of promise the immutability of his counsel, confirmed it by an oath: 18 That by two immutable things, in that it was impossible for God to lie, we might have strong encouragement, who have fled for refuge to lay hold upon the hope set before us: 19 **Which hope we have as an anchor of the soul**, both sure and steadfast, and which enters into that within the veil; 20 Where the forerunner is for us entered, even Jesus, made a high priest forever after the order of Melchizedek.

7:25 Therefore **he is able also to save them to the uttermost that come unto God by him**, seeing he ever lives to make intercession for them.

8:8 For finding fault with them (former laws), he says, Behold, the days come, says the Lord, when **I will make a new covenant with the house of Israel** and with the house of Judah: 9 Not according to the covenant that I made with their fathers in the day when I took them by the hand to lead them out of the land of Egypt; because they continued not in my covenant, and I regarded them not, says the Lord. 10 For this is the covenant that I will make with the house of Israel after those days, says the Lord; **I will put my laws into their mind, and write them in their hearts: and I will be to them a God, and they shall be to me a people:** 11 And they shall not teach every man his neighbor, and every man his brother, saying, Know the Lord: for all shall know me, from the least to the greatest. 12 **For I will be merciful to their unrighteousness, and their sins and their iniquities will I remember no more.**

9:11 But Christ being come a high priest of good things to come, by a greater and more perfect tabernacle, not made with hands, that is to say, not of this building; 12 Neither by the blood of goats and calves, but **by his own blood he entered in once into the holy place, having obtained eternal redemption for us.** 13 For if the blood of bulls and of goats, and the ashes of a heifer sprinkling the unclean, sanctifies to the purifying of the flesh: 14 How much more shall the blood of Christ, who through the eternal Spirit offered himself without spot to God, purge your conscience from dead works to serve the living God? 15 And for this cause **he is the mediator of the new covenant, that by means of death, for the redemption of the transgressions that were under the first covenant, they who are called might receive the promise of eternal inheritance.**

9:26 For then must he often have suffered since the foundation of the world: **but now once in the end of the age has he appeared to put away sin by the sacrifice of himself.** 27 And as it is appointed unto men once to die, but after this the judgment: 28 **So Christ was once offered to bear the sins of many**; and unto them that look for him shall he appear the second time without sin unto salvation.

10:9 Then said he, Lo, I come to do your will, O God. **He takes away the first, that he may establish the second.** 10 By the which will **we are sanctified through the offering of the body of Jesus Christ once for all.**

10:14 For by one offering he has perfected forever them that are sanctified.

10:16 This is the covenant that I will make with them after those days, says the Lord, I will put my laws into their hearts, and in their minds will I write them; 17 And their sins and iniquities will I remember no more.

10:19 Having therefore, brethren, boldness to enter into the holiest by the blood of Jesus, 20 By a new and living way, which he has consecrated for us, through the veil, that is to say, his flesh; 21 And having a high priest over the house of God; 22 **Let us draw near with a true heart in full assurance of faith, having our hearts sprinkled from an evil conscience**, and our bodies washed with pure water.

11:1 Now faith is the substance of things hoped for, the evidence of things not seen.

11:6 But without faith it is impossible to please him: for he that comes to God must believe that he is, and that **he is a rewarder of them that diligently seek him**.

12:28 Therefore **we receiving a kingdom which cannot be moved, let us have grace**, by which we may serve God acceptably with reverence and godly fear: 9 Be not carried about with various and strange doctrines. For **it is a good thing that the heart be established with grace**; not with foods, which have not profited them that have been observing them.

13:8 Jesus Christ the same yesterday, and today, and forever.

13:20 Now the God of peace, that brought again from the dead our Lord Jesus, that great shepherd of the sheep, through the blood of the everlasting covenant, 21 **Make you complete in every good work to do his will, working in you that which is well pleasing in his sight**, through Jesus Christ; to whom be glory forever and ever. Amen.

JAMES

1:4 But let patience have her perfect work, that you may be perfect and entire, lacking in nothing. 5 **If any of you lacks wisdom, let him ask of God, who gives to all men liberally**, and reproaches not; and it shall be given him.

1:12 Blessed is the man that endures trial: for when he is tried, **he shall receive the crown of life**, which the Lord has promised to them that love him.

1:13 Let no man say when he is tempted, I am tempted of God: for God cannot be tempted with evil, neither tempts he any man:

1:17 Every good gift and every perfect gift is from above, and comes down from the Father of lights, with whom is no variableness, neither shadow of turning.

1:25 But whoever looks into the perfect law of liberty, and continues in it, he being not a forgetful hearer, but a doer of the work, **this man shall be blessed in his deed.**

2:5 Hearken, my beloved brethren, **Has not God chosen the poor of this world rich in faith, and heirs of the kingdom which he has promised to them that love him?**

4:6 But **he gives more grace**. Therefore he says, God resists the proud, but **gives grace unto the humble**. 7 Submit yourselves therefore to God. Resist the devil, and he will flee from you. 8 **Draw near to God, and he will draw near to you.** Cleanse your hands, you sinners; and purify your hearts, you double-minded.

5:14 Is any sick among you? let him call for the elders of the church; and let them pray over him, anointing him with oil in the name of the Lord: 15 And **the prayer of faith shall deliver the sick, and the Lord shall raise him up**; and if he has committed sins, they shall be forgiven him.

5:20 Let him know, that he who converts the sinner from the error of his way shall save a soul from death, and shall hide a multitude of sins.

I PETER

1:3 Blessed be the God and Father of our Lord Jesus Christ, who according to his abundant mercy **has begotten us again unto a living hope** by the resurrection of Jesus Christ from the dead, 4 To **an inheritance incorruptible**, and undefiled, and **that fades not away**, reserved in heaven for you, 5 Who are **kept by the power of God through faith** unto salvation ready to be revealed in the last time.

1:18 Since you know that you were not redeemed with corruptible things, as silver and gold, from your vain manner of life received by tradition from your fathers; 19 But **with the precious blood of Christ, as of a lamb without blemish and without spot**: 20 Who verily was foreordained before the foundation of the world, but was manifest in these last times for you, 21 Who **by him do believe in God**, that raised him up from the dead, and gave him glory; that **your faith and hope might be in God**.

1:25 But **the word of the Lord endures forever**. And this is the word which by the gospel is preached unto you.

2:9 But you are a chosen generation, a royal priesthood, a holy nation, a people for his own; that you should show forth the praises of him who has called you out of darkness into his marvelous light: 10 Who in time past were not a people, but are now the people of God: who had not obtained mercy, but now have obtained mercy.

2:24 Who **his own self bore our sins in his own body on the tree, that we, being dead to sins, should live unto righteousness: by whose stripes you were healed.** 25 For you were as sheep going astray; but are **now returned unto the Shepherd and Bishop of your souls.**

3:12 **For the eyes of the Lord are over the righteous, and his ears are open unto their prayers**: but the face of the Lord is against them that do evil.

3:18 For Christ also has once suffered for sins, the just for the unjust, that he might bring us to God, being put to death in the flesh, but made alive by the Spirit

5:4 And when the chief Shepherd shall appear, **you shall receive a crown of glory that fades not away**.

5:7 Casting all your care upon him; for he cares for you.

5:10 But the God of all grace, who has called us unto his eternal glory by Christ Jesus, after that you have suffered a while, restore, establish, strengthen, settle you.

II PETER

1:2 **Grace and peace be multiplied unto you through the knowledge of God, and of Jesus our Lord,**3 According as his divine power has given unto us all things that pertain unto life and godliness, through the knowledge of him who has called us to glory and virtue: 4 **By which are given unto us exceedingly great and precious promises: that by these you might be partakers of the divine nature**, having escaped the corruption that is in the world through lust.

3:9 The Lord is not slack concerning his promise, as some men count slackness; but is longsuffering toward us, not willing that any should perish, but that all should come to repentance.

3:13 Nevertheless we, according to his promise, look for new heavens and a new earth, in which dwells righteousness.

I JOHN

1:2 (For the life was manifested, and we have seen it, and bear witness, and show unto you that eternal life, which was with the Father, and was manifested unto us;)

1:7 But if we walk in the light, as he is in the light, we have fellowship one with another, and the blood of Jesus Christ his Son cleanses us from all sin.

1:9 If we confess our sins, he is faithful and just to forgive us our sins, and to cleanse us from all unrighteousness.

2:1 My little children, these things write I unto you, that you sin not. And if any man sin, we have an advocate with the Father, Jesus Christ the righteous: 2 And he is the propitiation for our sins: and not for ours only, but also for the sins of the whole world.

2:12 I write unto you, little children, because your sins are forgiven you for his name's sake.

2:17 And the world passes away, and the lust thereof: but he that does the will of God abides forever.

2:20 But **you have an anointing from the Holy One**, and you know all things.

2:25 And this is the promise that he has promised us, even eternal life.

2:27 But **the anointing which you have received of him abides in you**, and you need not that any man teach you: but as the same anointing teaches you of all things, and is truth, and is no lie, and even as it has taught you, you shall abide in him.

3:1 Behold, what manner of love the Father has bestowed upon us, that **we should be called the children of God**: therefore the world knows us not, because it knew him not. 2 Beloved, **now are we the children of God**, and it does not yet appear what we shall be: but we know that, when he shall appear, we shall be like him; for we shall see him as he is. 3 And every man that has this hope in him purifies himself, even as he is pure.

3:21 Beloved, if our heart condemns us not, then have we confidence toward God. 22 And whatsoever we ask, we receive of him, because we keep his commandments, and do those things that are pleasing in his sight. 23 And this is his commandment, That we should believe on the name of his Son Jesus Christ, and love one another, as he gave us commandment.

4:9 In this was manifested the love of God toward us, because **God sent his only begotten Son into the world, that we might live through him.** 10 In this is love, not that we loved God, but that he loved us, and sent his Son to be the propitiation for our sins.

4:13 By this we know that we dwell in him, and he in us, because **he has given us of his Spirit.**

4:16 And we have known and believed the love that God has for us. God is love; and he that dwells in love dwells in God, and God in him. 17 In this is our love made perfect, that **we may have boldness in the day of judgment: because as he is, so are we in this world. 18 There is no fear in love; but perfect love casts out fear: because fear has to do with punishment. He that fears is not made perfect in love.**

4:19 We love him, because he first loved us.

5:1 Whosoever believes that Jesus is the Christ is born of God: and everyone that loves him that begat loves him also that is begotten of him.

5:4 For whoever is born of God overcomes the world: and this is the victory that overcomes the world, even our faith.

5:13 These things have I written unto you that believe on the name of the Son of God; that you may know that you have eternal life, and that you may believe on the name of the Son of God. 14 And this is the confidence that we have in him, that, if we ask anything according to his will, he hears us: 15 And if we know that he hears us, whatsoever we ask, we know that we have the requests that we desired of him.

II JOHN

2 For the truth's sake, which dwells in us, and shall be with us forever. 3 Grace be with you, mercy, and peace, from God the Father, and from the Lord Jesus Christ, the Son of the Father, in truth and love.

III JOHN

2 Beloved, I wish above all things that you may prosper and be in health, even as your soul prospers.

JUDE

20 But you, beloved, building up yourselves in your most holy faith, praying in the Holy Spirit, 21 Keep yourselves in the love of God, looking for the mercy of our Lord Jesus Christ unto eternal life.

24 Now unto him who is able to keep you from falling, and to present you faultless before the presence of his glory with exceeding joy, 25 To the only wise God our Savior, be glory and majesty, dominion and power, both now and forever. Amen.

REVELATION

1:3 Blessed is he that reads, and they that hear the words of this prophecy, and keep those things which are written therein: for the time is at hand.

1:5 And from Jesus Christ, who is the faithful witness, and the first begotten of the dead, and the prince of the kings of the earth. Unto him that loves us, and **washed us from our sins in his own blood**, 6 And has **made us a kingdom and priests unto God and his Father**; to him be glory and dominion forever and ever. Amen.

1:18 I am he that lives, and was dead; and, behold, I am alive forevermore, Amen; and have the keys of hades and of death.

3:20 Behold, I stand at the door, and knock: **if any man hears my voice, and opens the door, I will come in to him, and will eat with him, and he with me**. 21 To him that overcomes will I grant to sit with me in my throne, even as I also overcame, and sat down with my Father in his throne.

5:9 And they sang a new song, saying, You are worthy to take the scroll, and to open the seals thereof: for you were slain, and **have redeemed us to God by your blood** out of every tribe, and tongue, and people, and nation; 10 And have **made us unto our God a kingdom and priests: and we shall reign on the earth**.

7:16 They shall hunger no more, neither thirst any more; neither shall the sun strike them, nor any heat. 17 For the Lamb who is in the midst of the throne shall feed them, and shall lead them unto living fountains of waters: and God shall wipe away all tears from their eyes.

11:15 And the seventh angel sounded; and there were great voices in heaven, saying, **The kingdom of this world has become the** kingdom of our Lord, and of his Christ; and he shall reign forever and ever.

20:6 **Blessed and holy is he that has part in the first resurrection**: on **such the second death has no power**, but they shall be priests of God and of Christ, and shall reign with him a thousand years.

21:4 And God shall wipe away all tears from their eyes; and there shall be no more death, neither sorrow, nor crying, neither shall there be any more pain: for the former things are passed away.

21:6 And he said unto me, It is done. I am Alpha and Omega, the beginning and the end. **I will give unto him that is thirsty of the fountain of the water of life freely. 7 He that overcomes shall inherit all things; and I will be his God, and he shall be my son.**

22:3 And there shall be no more curse: but the throne of God and of the Lamb shall be in it; and his servants shall serve him:

22:17 And the Spirit and the bride say, Come. And let him that hears say, Come. And let him that is thirsty come. **And whosoever will, let him take the water of life freely.**

PROMISES FROM THE OLD TESTAMENT

No matter how many promises are made, they are yes and amen in Christ. Keep in mind that Christ has fulfilled the Law for righteousness and you are in him. His faithfulness qualifies you for any and all promises, not your ability to keep the Law or remain faithful. Now it's up to you to believe in your heart that you are in him and he **is** your righteousness. Remember that you are a joint-heir with Jesus as you read through these Old Testament promises.

REMEMBER!! Under the Old the promises were available "if you," now, in Christ they are available "for you."

GENESIS

1:26 And God said, Let us make man in our image, after our likeness: and let them have dominion over the fish of the sea, and over the fowl of the air, and over the cattle, and over all the earth, and over every creeping thing that creeps upon the earth. 27 So God created man in his own image, in the image of God created he him; male and female created he them. 28 And God blessed them, and God said unto them, Be fruitful, and multiply, and fill the earth, and subdue it: and have dominion over the fish of the sea, and over the fowl of the air, and over every living thing that moves upon the earth.

8:21 And the LORD smelled a sweet odor; and the LORD said in his heart, I will not again curse the ground any more for man's sake; for the imagination of man's heart is evil from his youth; neither will I again smite any more everything living, as I have done. 22 While the earth remains, seedtime and harvest, and cold and heat, and summer and winter, and day and night shall not cease.

9:1 And God blessed Noah and his sons, and said unto them, Be fruitful, and multiply, and fill the earth.

12:2 And I will make of you a great nation, and I will bless you, and make your name great; and you shall be a blessing: 3 And I will bless them that bless you, and curse him that curses you: and in you shall all families of the earth be blessed.

17:1 And when Abram was ninety years old and nine, the LORD appeared to Abram, and said unto him, I am the Almighty God; walk before me, and be you perfect. 2 And I will make my covenant between me and you, and will multiply you exceedingly. 3 And Abram fell on his face: and God talked with him, saying, 4 As for me, behold, my covenant is with you, and you shall be a father of many nations. 5 Neither shall your name any more be called Abram, but your name shall be Abraham; for a father of many nations have I made you. 6 And I will make you exceedingly fruitful, and I will make nations of you, and kings shall come out of you. 7 And I will establish my covenant between me and you and your descendants after you in their generations for an everlasting covenant, to be a God unto you, and to your descendants after you. 8 And I will give unto you, and to your descendants after you, the land in which you are a sojourner, all the land of Canaan, for an everlasting possession; and I will be their God.

18:14 Is anything too hard for the LORD? At the time appointed I will return unto you, according to the time of life, and Sarah shall have a son.

18:19 For I know him, that he will command his children and his household after him, and they shall keep the way of the LORD, to do righteousness and justice; that the LORD may bring upon Abraham that which he has spoken of him.

22:17 That in blessing I will bless you, and in multiplying I will multiply your descendants as the stars of the heaven, and as the sand which is upon the seashore; and your descendants shall possess the gate of their enemies; 18 And in your descendants shall all the nations of the earth be blessed; because you have obeyed my voice.

EXODUS

6:7 And I will take you to me for a people, and I will be to you a God: and ye shall know that I am the LORD your God, which bringeth you out from under the burdens of the Egyptians.

9:16 And in very deed for this cause have I raised thee up, for to shew in thee my power; and that my name may be declared throughout all the earth.

19:5-6 Now therefore, if ye will obey my voice indeed, and keep my covenant, then ye shall be a peculiar treasure unto me above all people: for all the earth is mine: And ye shall be unto me a kingdom of priests, and an holy nation. These are the words which thou shalt speak unto the children of Israel.

33:14 And he said, My presence shall go with thee, and I will give thee rest.

34:6-7 And the LORD passed by before him, and proclaimed, The LORD, The LORD God, merciful and gracious, longsuffering, and abundant in goodness and truth, Keeping mercy for thousands, forgiving iniquity and transgression and sin, and that will by no means clear the guilty; visiting the iniquity of the fathers upon the children, and upon the children's children, unto the third and to the fourth generation.

LEVITICUS

10:3 Then Moses said to Aaron, "This is what the LORD has said: 'Among those who are near me I will be sanctified, and before all the people I will be glorified.'" And Aaron held his peace.

11:44 For I am the LORD your God. Consecrate yourselves therefore, and be holy, for I am holy. You shall not defile yourselves with any swarming thing that crawls on the ground. 45 For I am the LORD who brought you up out of the land of Egypt to be your God. You shall therefore be holy, for I am holy."

17:11 For the life of the flesh is in the blood, and I have given it for you on the altar to make atonement for your souls, for it is the blood that makes atonement by the life.

18:5 You shall therefore keep my statutes and my rules; if a person does them, he shall live by them: I am the LORD.

20:26 You shall be holy to me, for I the LORD am holy and have separated you from the peoples, that you should be mine.

26:12 And I will walk among you and will be your God, and you shall be my people. 13 I am the LORD your God, who brought you out of the land of Egypt, that you should not be their slaves. And I have broken the bars of your yoke and made you walk erect.

NUMBERS

6:24 The LORD bless you and keep you; 25 the LORD make his face to shine upon you and be gracious to you; 26 the LORD lift up his countenance upon you and give you peace.

11:23 And the LORD said to Moses, "Is the LORD's hand shortened? Now you shall see whether my word will come true for you or not."

14:17 And now, please let the power of the Lord be great as you have promised, saying, 18 'The LORD is slow to anger and abounding in steadfast love, forgiving iniquity and transgression, but he will by no means clear the guilty, visiting the iniquity of the fathers on the children, to the third and the fourth generation.' 19 Please pardon the iniquity of this people, according to the greatness of your steadfast love, just as you have forgiven this people, from Egypt until now."

15:41 I am the Lord your God, who brought you out of Egypt to be your God. I am the Lord your God

23:19 God is not man, that he should lie, or a son of man, that he should change his mind. Has he said, and will he not do it? Or has he spoken, and will he not fulfill it?

DEUTERONOMY

1:10-11 The Lord your God has increased your numbers so that today you are as many as the stars in the sky. May the Lord, the God of your fathers, increase you a thousand times and bless you as he has promised!

1:30-31 **The Lord your God, who is going before you, will fight for you,** as he did for you in Egypt, before your very eyes, and in the desert. There you saw how the Lord your God carried you, as a father carries his son, all the way you went until you reached this place

2:7 The Lord your God has blessed you in all the work of your hands. He has watched over your journey through this vast desert. These forty years the Lord your God has been with you, and you have not lacked anything

3:22 Do not be afraid of them; the Lord your God himself will fight for you.

4:7 What other nation is so great as to have their gods near them the way the Lord our God is near us whenever we pray to him?

4:29 If you seek the Lord your God, you will find him if you look for him with all your heart and with all your soul

4:31 For the Lord your God is a merciful God; he will not abandon or destroy you or forget the covenant with your forefathers, which he confirmed to them by oath.

7:9 The Lord is God; he is the faithful God, keeping his covenant of love to a thousand generations of those who love him and keep his commands.

20:4 The Lord your God is the one who goes with you to fight for you against your enemies to give you victory.

29:29 The secret things belong to the Lord our God, but the things revealed belong to us and to our children forever.

JOSHUA

1:8 Study this Book of Instruction continually. Meditate on it day and night so you will be sure to obey everything written in it. Only then will you prosper and succeed in all you do.

1:9 This is my command—be strong and courageous! Do not be afraid or discouraged. For the LORD your God is with you wherever you go."

2:11 No wonder our hearts have melted in fear! No one has the courage to fight after hearing such things. For the LORD your God is the supreme God of the heavens above and the earth below.

21:43 So the LORD gave to Israel all the land he had sworn to give their ancestors, and they took possession of it and settled there. 44 And the LORD gave them rest on every side, just as he had solemnly promised their ancestors. None of their enemies could stand against them, for the LORD helped them conquer all their enemies. 45 **Not a single one of all the good promises the LORD had given to the family of Israel was left unfulfilled; everything he had spoken came true**.

23:14 "Now I am about to go the way of all the earth. You know with all your heart and soul that not one of all the good promises the Lord your God gave you has failed. Every promise has been fulfilled; not one has failed.

JUDGES

3:15 Again the Israelites cried out to the Lord, and he gave them a deliverer—Ehud, a left-handed man, the son of Gera the Benjamite. The Israelites sent him with tribute to Eglon king of Moab.

RUTH

2:12 May the Lord repay you for what you have done. May you be richly rewarded by the Lord, the God of Israel, under whose wings you have come to take refuge

4:14 The women said to Naomi: "Praise be to the Lord, who this day has not left you without a guardian-redeemer. May he become famous throughout Israel! 15 **He will renew your life and sustain you in your old age**. For your daughter-in-law, who loves you and who is better to you than seven sons, has given him birth."

I SAMUEL

2:2 There is no one holy like the Lord; there is no one besides you; there is no Rock like our God.

2:9 He will guard the feet of his faithful servants, but the wicked will be silenced in the place of darkness. "It is not by strength that one prevails;

2:30 "Therefore the Lord, the God of Israel, declares: 'I promised that members of your family would minister before me forever.' But now the Lord declares: 'Far be it from me! Those who honor me I will honor, but those who despise me will be disdained.

7:3 So Samuel said to all the Israelites, "If you are returning to the Lord with all your hearts, then rid yourselves of the foreign gods and the Ashtoreths and commit yourselves to the Lord and serve him only, and he will deliver you out of the hand of the Philistines."

14:6 Jonathan said to his young armor-bearer, "Come, let's go over to the outpost of those uncircumcised men. Perhaps the Lord will act in our behalf. **Nothing can hinder the Lord from saving, whether by many or by few.**"

15:29 He who is the Glory of Israel does not lie or change his mind; **for he is not a human being, that he should change his mind.**"

16:7 But the Lord said to Samuel, "Do not consider his appearance or his height, for I have rejected him. **The Lord does not look at the things people look at. People look at the outward appearance, but the Lord looks at the heart.**"

17:47 All those gathered here will know that it is not by sword or spear that the Lord saves; for the battle is the Lord's, and he will give all of you into our hands."

26:23 The Lord rewards everyone for their righteousness and faithfulness. The Lord delivered you into my hands today, but I would not lay a hand on the Lord's anointed. 24 As surely as I valued your life today, so may the Lord value my life and deliver me from all trouble."

II SAMUEL

7:11b "'The Lord declares to you that **the Lord himself will establish a house for you:** 12 When your days are over and you rest with your ancestors, I will raise up your offspring to succeed you, your own flesh and blood, and I will establish his kingdom. 13 He is the one who will build a house for my Name, and I will establish the throne of his kingdom forever.

7:16 Your house and your kingdom will endure forever before me; your throne will be established forever.

7:24 You have established your people Israel as your very own forever, and you, Lord, have become their God.

7:28 And now, O Lord GOD, you are God, and your words are true, and you have promised this good thing to your servant.

10:12 Be of good courage, and let us be courageous for our people, and for the cities of our God, and may the LORD do what seems good to him.

14:14 We must all die; we are like water spilled on the ground, which cannot be gathered up again. But God will not take away life, and he devises means so that the banished one will not remain an outcast.

22:4 I call upon the LORD, who is worthy to be praised, and I am saved from my enemies.

22:31 This God—his way is perfect; the word of the LORD proves true; he is a shield for all those who take refuge in him. 32 "For who is God, but the LORD? And who is a rock, except our God? 33 This God is my strong refuge and has made my way blameless.

I KINGS

2:2 "I am about to go the way of all the earth. Be strong, and show yourself a man, 3 and keep the charge of the LORD your God, walking in his ways and keeping his statutes, his commandments, his rules, and his testimonies, as it is written in the Law of Moses, **that you may prosper in all that you do and wherever you turn**

8:23 and said, "O LORD, God of Israel, there is no God like you, in heaven above or on earth beneath, keeping covenant and showing steadfast love to your servants who walk before you with all their heart

8:56 "Blessed be the LORD who has given rest to his people Israel, according to all that he promised. Not one word has failed of all his good promise, which he spoke by Moses his servant. 57 The LORD our God be with us, as he was with our fathers. May he not leave us or forsake us, 58 that he may incline our hearts to him, to walk in all his ways and to keep his commandments, his statutes, and his rules, which he commanded our fathers.

II KINGS

6:16 He said, "Do not be afraid, for those who are with us are more than those who are with them."

8:19 Yet the LORD was not willing to destroy Judah, for the sake of David his servant, since he promised to give a lamp to him and to his sons forever.

13:23 But the LORD was gracious to them and had compassion on them, and he turned toward them, because of his covenant with Abraham, Isaac, and Jacob, and would not destroy them, nor has he cast them from his presence until now.

17:39 but you shall fear the LORD your God, and he will deliver you out of the hand of all your enemies.

I CHRONICLES

4:10 Jabez called upon the God of Israel, saying, "Oh that you would bless me and enlarge my border, and that your hand might be with me, and that **you would keep me from harm so that it might not bring me pain!**" And God granted what he asked.

16:10 Glory in his holy name; let the hearts of those who seek the LORD rejoice! 11 Seek the LORD and his strength; seek his presence continually! 12 Remember the wondrous works that he has done, his miracles and the judgments he uttered, 13 O offspring of Israel his servant, children of Jacob, his chosen ones!

16:25 For great is the LORD, and greatly to be praised, and he is to be feared above all gods. 26 For all the gods of the peoples are worthless idols, but the LORD made the heavens. 27 Splendor and majesty are before him; strength and joy are in his place.

16:34 Oh give thanks to the LORD, for he is good; for his steadfast love endures forever!

17:10 from the time that I appointed judges over my people Israel. And I will subdue all your enemies. Moreover, I declare to you that the LORD will build you a house. 11 When your days are fulfilled to walk with your fathers, I will raise up your offspring after you, one of your own sons, and I will establish his kingdom. 12 He shall build a house for me, and I will establish his throne forever. 13 I will be to him a father, and he shall be to me a son. I will not take my steadfast love from him, as I took it from him who was before you, 14 but I will confirm him in my house and in my kingdom forever, and his throne shall be established forever.

17:20 There is none like you, O LORD, and there is no God besides you, according to all that we have heard with our ears. 21 And who is like your people Israel, the one nation on earth whom God went to redeem to be his people, making for yourself a name for great and awesome things, in driving out nations before your people whom you redeemed from Egypt? 22 And you made your people Israel to be your people forever, and you, O LORD, became their God.

22:9 Behold, a son shall be born to you who shall be a man of rest. I will give him rest from all his surrounding enemies. For his name shall be Solomon, and I will give peace and quiet to Israel in his days. 10 He shall build a house for my name. He shall be my son, and I will be his father, and I will establish his royal throne in Israel forever.'

29:14 "But who am I, and what is my people, that we should be able thus to offer willingly? For all things come from you, and of your own have we given you.

II CHRONICLES

6:14-15 O Lord, God of Israel, there is no God like you in heaven or on earth—you who keep your covenant of love with your servants who continue wholeheartedly in your way. You have kept your promise to your servant David my father; with your mouth you have promised and with your hand you have fulfilled it—as it is today

14:11 Then Asa called to the Lord his God and said, 'Lord, there is no one like you to help the powerless against the mighty. Help us, O Lord our God, for we rely on you, and in your name we have come against this vast army. O Lord, you are our God; do not let man prevail against you'

15:2 The Lord is with you when your are with him. If you seek him, he will be found by you, but if you forsake him, he will forsake you

15:4 In their distress they turned to the Lord, the God of Israel, and sought him, and he was found by them.

15:7 As for you, be strong and do not give up, for your work will be rewarded

16:9 The eyes of the Lord range throughout the earth to strengthen those whose hearts are fully committed to him

19:7 Now let the fear of the Lord be upon you. Judge carefully, for with the Lord our God there is no injustice or partiality or bribery

20:15 Do not be afraid or discouraged because of this vast army. For the battle is not yours, but God's

20:20 Have faith in the Lord your God and you will be upheld; have faith in his prophets and you will be successful

30:9 The Lord your God is gracious and compassionate. He will not turn his face from you if you return to him

32:7-8 Do not be afraid or discouraged because of the king of Assyria and the vast army with him, for there is a greater power with us than with him. With him is only the arm of flesh, but with us is the Lord our God to help us and to fight our battles

EZRA

8:22 The good hand of our God is on everyone who looks to him, but his great anger is against all who forsake him

9:8-9 But now, for a brief moment, the Lord our God has been gracious in leaving us a remnant and giving us a firm place in his sanctuary, and so our God gives light to our eyes and a little relief in our bondage. Though we are slaves, our God has not deserted us in our bondage. He has shown us kindness in the sight of the kings of Persia: He has granted us new life to rebuild the house of our God and repair its ruins, and he has given us a wall of protection in Judah and Jerusalem

NEHEMIAH

1:5-6 O Lord, God of heaven, the great and awesome God, who keeps his covenant of love with those who love him and obey his commands, let your ear be attentive and your eyes open to hear the prayer your servant is praying before you day and night for your servants, the people of Israel

2:20 The God of heaven will give us success. We his servants will start rebuilding.

4:14 Don't be afraid of them. Remember the Lord, who is great and awesome, and fight for your brothers, your sons and your daughters, your wives and your homes.

8:10 This day is sacred to our Lord. Do not grieve, for the joy of the Lord is your strength.

9:5-6 Blessed be your glorious name, and may it be exalted above all blessing and praise. You alone are the Lord. You made the heavens, even the highest heavens, and all their starry host, the earth and all that is on it, the seas and all that is in them. You give life to everything, and the multitudes of heaven worship you.

9:8 You have kept your promise because you are righteous.

ESTHER

4:13-14 Do not think that because you are in the king's house you alone of all the Jews will escape. For if you remain silent at this time, relief and deliverance for the Jews will arise from another place, but you and your father's family will perish. And who knows but that you have come to royal position for such a time as this?

8:16 For the Jews it was a time of happiness and joy, gladness and honor.

JOB

5:17 Blessed is the man whom God corrects; so do not despise the discipline of the Almighty.

10:12 You gave me life and showed me kindness, and in your providence watched over my spirit.

12:13-14 To God belong wisdom and power; counsel and understanding are his. What he tears down cannot be rebuilt; the man he imprisons cannot be released.

14:14 If a man dies, will he live again? All the days of my hard service I will wait for my renewal to come.

16:19 Even now my witness is in heaven; my advocate is on high.

19:25-27 I know that my Redeemer lives, and that in the end he will stand upon the earth. And after my skin has been destroyed, yet in my flesh I will see God; I myself will see him with my own eyes—

37:23-24 The Almighty is beyond our reach and exalted in power; in his justice and great righteousness, he does not oppress. Therefore, men revere him, for does he not have regard for all the wise in heart?

42:2 I know that you can do all things; no plan of yours can be thwarted

PSALMS

1:1-3 Blessed is the man who does not walk in the counsel of the wicked or stand in the way of sinners or sit in the seat of mockers. But his delight is in the law of the Lord, and on his law he meditates day and night. He is like a tree planted by streams of water, which yields its fruit in season and whose leaf does not wither. Whatever he does prospers.

2:12 Blessed are all who take refuge in him

4:3 Know that the Lord has set apart the godly for himself; the Lord will hear when I call to him

5:12 For surely, O Lord, you bless the righteous; you surround them with your favor as with a shield

9:9-10 The Lord is a refuge for the oppressed, a stronghold in times of trouble. Those who know your name will trust in you, for you, Lord, have never forsaken those who seek you

9:9-10 The Lord is righteous, he loves justice; upright men will see his face

18:30 As for God, his way is perfect; the word of the Lord is flawless. He is a shield for all who take refuge in him

25:12 Who, then, is the man that fears the Lord? He will instruct him in the way chosen for him

25:12 I will instruct you and teach you in the way you should go; I will counsel you and watch over you

32:10 Many are the woes of the wicked, but the Lord's unfailing love surrounds the man who trusts in him

34:22 The Lord redeems his servants; no one who takes refuge in him will be condemned

37:4 Delight yourself in the Lord and he will give you the desires of your heart

55:22 Cast your cares on the Lord and he will sustain you; he will never let the righteous fall

84:11-12 The Lord bestows favor and honor; no good thing does he withhold from those whose walk is blameless. O Lord Almighty, blessed is the man who trusts in you

103:11-12 As high as the heavens are above the earth, so great is his love for those who fear him; as far as the east is from the west, so far has he removed our transgressions from us

121:8 The Lord will watch over your coming and going both now and forevermore

145:17-20 The Lord is righteous in all his ways and loving toward all he has made. The Lord is near to all who call on him, to all who call on him in truth. He fulfills the desires of those who fear him; he hears their cry and saves them. The Lord watches over all who love him, but all the wicked he will destroy

PROVERBS

1:7 The fear of the Lord is the beginning of knowledge, but fools despise wisdom and discipline

2:6-8 The Lord gives wisdom, and from his mouth come knowledge and understanding. He holds victory in store for the upright, he is a shield to those whose walk is blameless, for he guards the course of the just and protects the way of his faithful ones

3:5-6 Trust in the Lord with all your heart and lean not on your own understanding; in all your ways acknowledge him, and he will make your paths straight

3:11-12 My son, do not despise the Lord's discipline and do not resent his rebuke, because the Lord disciplines those he loves, as a father the son he delights in

8:17 I love those who love me, and those who seek me diligently find me.

8:35 For whoever finds me finds life and obtains favor from the LORD

9:10 The fear of the Lord is the beginning of wisdom, and knowledge of the Holy One is understanding

14:27 The fear of the Lord is a fountain of life, turning a man from the snares of death

15:33 The fear of the Lord teaches a man wisdom, and humility comes before honor

16:3 Commit to the Lord whatever you do, and your plans will succeed

18:10 The name of the Lord is a strong tower; the righteous run to it and are safe

19:21 Many are the plans in a man's heart, but it is the Lord's purpose that prevails

19:23 The fear of the Lord leads to life: Then one rests content, untouched by trouble

21:30 There is no wisdom, no insight, no plan that can succeed against the Lord

22:4 Humility and the fear of the Lord bring wealth and honor and life

ECCLESIASTES

2:24 There is nothing better for a person than that he should eat and drink and find enjoyment in his toil. This also, I saw, is from the hand of God, 25 for apart from him who can eat or who can have enjoyment? 26 For to the one who pleases him God has given wisdom and knowledge and joy, but to the sinner he has given the business of gathering and collecting, only to give to one who pleases God. This also is vanity and a striving after wind.

3:11 He has made everything beautiful in its time. He has also set eternity in the hearts of men; yet they cannot fathom what God has done from beginning to end

3:14 I know that everything God does will endure forever; nothing can be added to it and nothing taken from it. God does it, so men will revere him

5:18-19 Then I realized that it is good and proper for a man to eat and drink, and to find satisfaction in his toilsome labor under the sun during the few days of life God has given him—for this is his lot. Moreover, when God gives any man wealth and possessions, and enables him to enjoy them, to accept his lot and be happy in his work—this is a gift of God.

8:12 Although a wicked man commits a hundred crimes and still lives a long time, I know that it will go better with God-fearing men, who are reverent before God

12:13-14 Now all has been heard; here is the conclusion of the matter: Fear God and keep his commandments, for this is the whole duty of man. For God will bring every deed into judgment, including every hidden thing, whether it is good or evil

SONG OF SONGS

2:4 He has taken me to the banquet hall, and his banner over me is love

2:16 My lover is mine and I am his

6:3 I am my lover's and my lover is mine

7:10 I belong to my lover, and his desire is for me

8:6 Set me as a seal upon your heart, as a seal upon your arm, for love is strong as death, jealousy is fierce as the grave. Its flashes are flashes of fire, the very flame of the LORD. 7 Many waters cannot quench love, neither can floods drown it. If a man offered for love all the wealth of his house, he would be utterly despised. 8We have a little sister, and she has no breasts. What shall we do for our sister on the day when she is spoken for? 9 If she is a wall, we will build on her a battlement of silver, but if she is a door, we will enclose her with boards of cedar.

ISAIAH

1:18 'Come now, let us reason together,' says the Lord. 'Though your sins are like scarlet, they shall be as white as snow; though they are red as crimson, they shall be like wool'

2:4 He will judge between the nations and will settle disputes for many peoples. They will beat their swords into plowshares and their spears into pruning hooks. Nation will not take up sword against nation, nor will they train for war anymore

4:2 In that day the Branch of the Lord will be beautiful and glorious, and the fruit of the land will be the pride and glory of the survivors in Israel

7:14 Therefore the Lord himself will give you a sign: The virgin will be with child and will give birth to a son, and will call him Immanuel

9:6-7 For to us a child is born, to us a son is given, and the government will be on his shoulders. And he will be called Wonderful Counselor, Mighty God, Everlasting Father, Prince of Peace. Of the increase of his government and peace there will be no end. He will reign on David's throne and over his kingdom, establishing and upholding it with justice and righteousness from that time on and forever

11:1-3 A shoot will come up from the stump of Jesse; from his roots a Branch will bear fruit. The Spirit of the Lord will rest on him—the Spirit of wisdom and of understanding, the Spirit of counsel and of power, the Spirit of knowledge and of the fear of the Lord—and he will delight in the fear of the Lord

11:6-9 The wolf will live with the lamb, the leopard will lie down with the goat, the calf and the lion and the yearling together; and a little child will lead them. The cow will feed with the bear, their young will lie down together, and the lion will eat straw like the ox. The infant will play near the hole of the cobra, and the young child put his hand into the viper's nest. They will neither harm nor destroy on all my holy mountain, for the earth will be full of the knowledge of the Lord as the waters cover the sea

12:2 Surely God is my salvation; I will trust and not be afraid. The Lord, the Lord, is my strength and my song; he has become my salvation

14:27 For the Lord Almighty has purposed, and who can thwart him? His hand is stretched out, and who can turn it back?

26:3 You will keep in perfect peace him whose mind is steadfast, because he trusts in you

30:15 In repentance and rest is your salvation, in quietness and trust is your strength

30:18 Yet the Lord longs to be gracious to you; he rises to show you compassion. For the Lord is a God of justice. Blessed are all who wait for him!

40:31 Those who hope in the Lord will renew their strength. They will soar on wings like eagles; they will run and not grow weary, they will walk and not be faint

41:10 Do not fear, for I am with you; do not be dismayed, for I am your God. I will strengthen you and help you; I will uphold you with my righteous right hand

48:17 I am the Lord your God, who teaches you what is best for you, who directs you in the way you should go

53:4-6 Surely he took up our infirmities and carried our sorrows, yet we considered him stricken by God, smitten by him, and afflicted. But he was pierced for our transgressions, he was crushed for our iniquities; the punishment that brought us peace was upon him, and by his wounds we are healed. We all, like sheep, have gone astray, each of us has turned to his own way; and the Lord has laid on him the iniquity of us all

54:4 Fear not; for thou shalt not be ashamed: neither be thou confounded; for thou shalt not be put to shame: for thou shalt forget the shame of thy youth, and shalt not remember the reproach of thy widowhood any more.

54:8-10 In a little wrath I hid my face from thee for a moment; but with everlasting kindness will I have mercy on thee, saith the LORD thy Redeemer. For this is as the waters of Noah unto me: for as I have sworn that the waters of Noah should no more go over the earth; so have I sworn that I would not be wroth with thee, nor rebuke thee. For the mountains shall depart, and the hills be removed; but my kindness shall not depart from thee, neither shall the covenant of my peace be removed, saith the LORD that hath mercy on thee.

57:15 I live in a high and holy place, but also with him who is contrite and lowly in spirit, to revive the spirit of the lowly and to revive the heart of the contrite

65:17 Behold, I will create new heavens and a new earth. The former things will not be remembered, nor will they come to mind

JEREMIAH

1:5 Before I formed you in the womb I knew you, before you were born I set you apart

3:17 At that time they will call Jerusalem The Throne of the Lord, and all nations will gather in Jerusalem to honor the name of the Lord. No longer will they follow the stubbornness of their evil hearts

7:5-7 If you really change your ways and your actions and deal with each other justly, if you do not oppress the alien, the fatherless or the widow and do not shed innocent blood in this place, and if you do not follow other gods to your own harm, then I will let you live in this place, in the land I gave your forefathers for ever and ever

7:23 Obey me, and I will be your God and you will be my people. Walk in all the ways I command you, that it may go well with you

9:23-24 Let not the wise man boast of his wisdom or the strong man boast of his strength or the rich man boast of his riches, but let him who boasts boast about this: that he understands and knows me, that I am the Lord, who exercises kindness, justice and righteousness on the earth, for in these I delight

10:23 I know, O Lord, that a man's life is not his own; it is not for men to direct his steps

12:15 After I uproot them, I will again have compassion and will bring each of them back to his own inheritance and his own country

17:7 "Blessed is the man who trusts in the LORD, whose trust is the LORD. 8 He is like a tree planted by water, that sends out its roots by the stream, and does not fear when heat comes, for its leaves remain green, and is not anxious in the year of drought, for it does not cease to bear fruit."

23:5-6 'The days are coming,' declares the Lord, 'when I will raise up to David a righteous Branch, a King who will reign wisely and do what is just and right in the land. In his days Judah will be saved and Israel will live in safety. This is the name by which he will be called: The Lord Our Righteousness

23:23-24 'Am I only a God nearby,' declares the Lord, 'and not a God far away? Can anyone hide in secret places so that I cannot see him?' declares the Lord. 'Do not I fill heaven and earth?' declares the Lord

24:6-7 My eyes will watch over them for their good, and I will bring them back to this land. I will build them up and not tear them down; I will plant them and not uproot them. I will give them a heart to know me, that I am the Lord. They will be my people, and I will be their God, for they will return to me with all their heart

29:11-13 'I know the plans I have for you,' declares the Lord, 'plans to prosper you and not to harm you, plans to give you hope and a future. Then you will call upon me and come and pray to me, and I will listen to you. You will seek me and find me when you seek me with all your heart'

31:33-34 'This is the covenant I will make with the house of Israel after that time,' declares the Lord. 'I will put my law in their minds and write it on their hearts. I will be their God, and they will be my people. No longer will a man teach his neighbor, or a man his brother, saying, "Know the Lord," because they will all know me, from the least of them to the greatest,' declares the Lord. 'For I will forgive their wickedness and will remember their sins no more'

33:3 Call to me and I will answer you and tell you great and unsearchable things you do not know

LAMENTATIONS

2:17 The Lord has done what he planned; he has fulfilled his word, which he decreed long ago

3:21-23 Yet this I call to mind and therefore I have hope: **Because of the Lord's great love we are not consumed,** for his compassions never fail. **They are new every morning; great is your faithfulness**

3:24-26 I say to myself, 'The Lord is my portion; therefore I will wait for him.' The Lord is good to those whose hope is in him, to the one who seeks him; it is good to wait quietly for the salvation of the Lord

3:32-33 Though he brings grief, he will show compassion, so great is his unfailing love. For he does not willingly bring affliction or grief to the children of men

3:37-38 Who can speak and have it happen if the Lord has not decreed it? Is it not from the mouth of the Most High that both calamities and good things come?

EZEKIEL

11:19-20 I will give them an undivided heart and put a new spirit in them; I will remove from them their heart of stone and give them a heart of flesh. Then they will follow my decrees and be careful to keep my laws. They will be my people, and I will be their God

18:32 Do I take any pleasure in the death of the wicked? Declares the Sovereign Lord. Rather, am I not pleased when they turn from their ways and live?

20:40 "For on My holy mountain, on the high mountain of Israel," declares the Lord GOD, "there the whole house of Israel, all of them, will serve Me in the land; there I will accept them and there I will seek your contributions and the choicest of your gifts, with all your holy things. 41 "As a soothing aroma I will accept you when I bring you out from the peoples and gather you from the lands where you are scattered; and I will prove Myself holy among you in the sight of the nations. 42 "And you will know that I am the LORD, when I bring you into the land of Israel, into the land which I swore to give to your forefathers. 43 "There you will remember your ways and all your deeds with which you have defiled yourselves; and you will loathe yourselves in your own sight for all the evil things that you have done. 44 "Then you will know that I am the LORD when I have dealt with you for My name's sake, not according to your evil ways or according to your corrupt deeds, O house of Israel," declares the Lord GOD."'

33:11 As surely as I live, declares the Sovereign Lord, I take no pleasure in the death of the wicked, but rather that they turn from their ways and live. Turn! Turn from your evil ways! Why will you die, O house of Israel?

34:11 For thus says the Lord GOD, "Behold, I Myself will search for My sheep and seek them out. 12 "As a shepherd cares for his herd in the day when he is among his scattered sheep, so I will care for My sheep and will deliver them from all the places to which they were scattered on a cloudy and gloomy day. 13 "I will bring them out from the peoples and gather them from the countries and bring them to their own land; and I will feed them on the mountains of Israel, by the streams, and in all the inhabited places of the land. 14 "I will feed them in a good pasture, and their grazing ground will be on the mountain heights of Israel. There they will lie down on good grazing ground and feed in rich pasture on the mountains of Israel. 15 "I will feed My flock and I will lead them to rest," declares the Lord GOD. 16 "I will seek the lost, bring back the scattered, bind up the broken and strengthen the sick; but the fat and the strong I will destroy. I will feed them with judgment.

34:23 "Then I will set over them one shepherd, My servant David, and he will feed them; he will feed them himself and be their shepherd. 24 "And I, the LORD, will be their God, and My servant David will be prince among them; I the LORD have spoken.

36:24 "For I will take you from the nations, gather you from all the lands and **bring you into your own land**. 25 "Then **I will sprinkle clean water on you, and you will be clean**; I will cleanse you from all your filthiness and from all your idols.

36:26 "Moreover, **I will give you a new heart and put a new spirit within you**; and I will remove the heart of stone from your flesh and give you a heart of flesh. 27 "**I will put My Spirit within you** and cause you to walk in My statutes, and you will be careful to observe My ordinances.

36:28 "You will live in the land that I gave to your forefathers; so you will be My people, and I will be your God. 29 "Moreover, I will save you from all your uncleanness; and I will call for the grain and multiply it, and I will not bring a famine on you. 30 "I will multiply the fruit of the tree and the produce of the field, so that you will not receive again the disgrace of famine among the nations.

37:13-14 Then you, my people, will know that I am the Lord, when I open your graves and bring you up from them. I will put my Spirit in you and you will live, and I will settle you in your own land

39:29 I will no longer hide my face from them, for I will pour out my Spirit on the house of Israel, declares the Sovereign Lord

DANIEL

2:20-22 Praise be to the name of God for ever and ever; wisdom and power are his. He changes times and seasons; he sets up kings and deposes them. He gives wisdom to the wise and knowledge to the discerning. He reveals deep and hidden things; he knows what lies in darkness, and light dwells with him

2:44 In the time of those kings, the God of heaven will set up a kingdom that will never be destroyed, nor will it be left to another people. It will crush all those kingdoms and bring them to an end, but it will itself endure forever

4:17 The Most High is sovereign over the kingdoms of men and gives them to anyone he wishes and sets over them the lowliest of men

4:34-35 Then I praised the Most High; I honored and glorified him who lives forever. His dominion is an eternal dominion; his kingdom endures from generation to generation. All the peoples of the earth are regarded as nothing. He does as he pleases with the powers of heaven and the peoples of the earth. No one can hold back his hand or say to him: 'What have you done?'

4:37 Now I, Nebuchadnezzar, praise and exalt and glorify the King of heaven, because everything he does is right and all his ways are just. And those who walk in pride he is able to humble

6:26-27 I issue a decree that in every part of my kingdom people must fear and reverence the God of Daniel. For he is the living God and he endures forever; his kingdom will not be destroyed, his dominion will never end. He rescues and saves; he performs signs and wonders in the heavens and on the earth

7:14 He was given authority, glory and sovereign power; all peoples, nations and men of every language worshiped him. His dominion is an everlasting dominion that will not pass away, and his kingdom is one that will never be destroyed

7:18 The saints of the Most High will receive the kingdom and will possess it forever—yes, for ever and ever

7:27 Then the sovereignty, power and greatness of the kingdoms under the whole heaven will be handed over to the saints, the people of the Most High. His kingdom will be an everlasting kingdom, and all rulers will worship and obey him

9:4 The Lord is "the great and awesome God, who keeps his covenant of love with all who love him and obey his commands

12:2-3 Multitudes who sleep in the dust of the earth will awake: some to everlasting life, others to shame and everlasting contempt. Those who are wise will shine like the brightness of the heavens, and those who lead many to righteousness, like the stars for ever and ever

HOSEA

1:7 I will show love to the house of Judah; and I will save them— not by bow, sword or battle, or by horses and horsemen, but by the Lord their God

1:10-11 The Israelites will be like the sand on the seashore, which cannot be measured or counted. In the place where it was said to them, 'You are not my people,' they will be called 'sons of the living God.' The people of Judah and the people of Israel will be reunited, and they will appoint one leader and will come up out of the land

2:19-20 I will betroth you to me forever; I will betroth you in righteousness and justice, in love and compassion. I will betroth you in faithfulness, and you will acknowledge the Lord

2:23 I will plant her for myself in the land; I will show my love to the one I called 'Not my loved one.' I will say to those called 'Not my people,' 'You are my people'; and they will say, 'You are my God'

6:6 I desire mercy, not sacrifice, and acknowledgment of God rather than burnt offerings

11:4 I led them with cords of human kindness, with ties of love; I lifted the yoke from their neck and bent down to feed them

11:9 I am God, and not man—the Holy One among you

13:14 I will ransom them from the power of the grave; I will redeem them from death. Where, O death, are your plagues? Where, O grave, is your destruction?

14:9 Who is wise? He will realize these things. Who is discerning? He will understand them. The ways of the Lord are right; the righteous walk in them, but the rebellious stumble in them

JOEL

2:13 Return to the Lord your God, for he is gracious and compassionate, slow to anger and abounding in love, and he relents from sending calamity

2:25-27 I will repay you for the years the locusts have eaten. You will have plenty to eat, until you are full, and you will praise the name of the Lord your God, who has worked wonders for you; never again will my people be shamed. Then you will know that I am in Israel, that I am the Lord your God, and that there is no other; never again will my people be shamed

2:28-32 I will pour out my Spirit on all people. Your sons and daughters will prophesy, your old men will dream dreams, your young men will see visions. Even on my servants, both men and women, I will pour out my Spirit in those days. I will show wonders in the heavens and on the earth, blood and fire and billows of smoke. The sun will be turned to darkness and the moon to blood before the coming of the great and dreadful day of the Lord. And everyone who calls on the name of the Lord will be saved

3:16-18 The Lord will roar from Zion and thunder from Jerusalem; the earth and the sky will tremble. But the Lord will be a refuge for his people, a stronghold for the people of Israel. Then you will know that I, the Lord your God, dwell in Zion, my holy hill. Jerusalem will be holy; never again will foreigners invade her. In that day the mountains will drip new wine, and the hills will flow with milk; all the ravines of Judah will run with water. A fountain will flow out of the Lord's house and will water the valley of acacias

AMOS

3:7-8 **Surely the Sovereign Lord does nothing without revealing his plan to his servants the prophets**. The lion has roared—who will not fear? The Sovereign Lord has spoken—who can but prophesy?

4:13 He who forms the mountains, creates the wind, and reveals his thoughts to man, he who turns dawn to darkness, and treads the high places of the earth—the Lord God Almighty is his name

5:8 He who made the Pleiades and Orion, who turns blackness into dawn and darkens day into night, who calls for the waters of the sea and pours them out over the face of the land—the Lord is his name

5:21-24 I hate, I despise your religious feasts; I cannot stand your assemblies. Even though you bring me burnt offerings and grain offerings, I will not accept them. Though you bring choice fellowship offerings, I will have no regard for them. Away with the noise of your songs! I will not listen to the music of your harps. But let justice roll on like a river, righteousness like a never-failing stream!

9:13-15 'The days are coming,' declares the Lord, 'when the reaper will be overtaken by the plowman and the planter by the one treading grapes. New wine will drip from the mountains and flow from all the hills. I will bring back my exiled people Israel; they will rebuild the ruined cities and live in them. They will plant vineyards and drink their wine; they will make gardens and eat their fruit. I will plant Israel in their own land, never again to be uprooted from the land I have given them,' says the Lord your God

OBADIAH

15 The day of the Lord is near for all nations. As you have done, it will be done to you; your deeds will return upon your own head

17-18 But on Mount Zion will be deliverance; it will be holy, and the house of Jacob will possess its inheritance. The house of Jacob will be a fire and the house of Joseph a flame; the house of Esau will be stubble, and they will set it on fire and consume it

21 Deliverers will go up on Mount Zion to govern the mountains of Esau. And the kingdom will be the Lord's

JONAH

2:2 In my distress I called to the Lord, and he answered me. From the depths of the grave I called for help, and you listened to my cry

2:7-9 When my life was ebbing away, I remembered you, Lord, and my prayer rose to you, to your holy temple. Those who cling to worthless idols forfeit the grace that could be theirs. But I, with a song of thanksgiving, will sacrifice to you. What I have vowed I will make good. Salvation comes from the Lord

4:2 I knew that you are a gracious and compassionate God, slow to anger and abounding in love, a God who relents from sending calamity

MICAH

2:7 "Do not my words do good to him who is upright?"

4:1-2 In the last days the mountain of the Lord's temple will be established as chief among the mountains; it will be raised above the hills, and peoples will stream to it. Many nations will come and say, 'Come, let us go up to the mountain of the Lord, to the house of the God of Jacob. He will teach us his ways so that we may walk in his paths.' The law will go out from Zion, the word of the Lord from Jerusalem

4:3 He will judge between many peoples and will settle disputes for strong nations far and wide. They will beat their swords into plowshares and their spears into pruning hooks. Nation will not take up sword against nation, nor will they train for war anymore

4:4-5 Every man will sit under his own vine and under his own fig tree, and no one will make them afraid, for the Lord Almighty has spoken. All the nations may walk in the name of their gods; we will walk in the name of the Lord our God for ever and ever

5:2 But you, Bethlehem Ephrathah, though you are small among the clans of Judah, out of you will come for me one who will be ruler over Israel, whose origins are from of old, from ancient times

5:4-5 He will stand and shepherd his flock in the strength of the Lord, in the majesty of the name of the Lord his God. And they will live securely, for then his greatness will reach to the ends of the earth. And he will be their peace

6:8 He has showed you, O man, what is good. And what does the Lord require of you? To act justly and to love mercy and to walk humbly with your God.

7:7 But as for me, I keep watch for the Lord, I wait in hope for God my Savior; my God will hear me

7:18-19 Who is a God like you, who pardons sin and forgives the transgression of the remnant of his inheritance? You do not stay angry forever but delight to show mercy. You will again have compassion on us; you will tread our sins underfoot and hurl all our iniquities into the depths of the sea

NAHUM

1:3 The Lord is slow to anger and great in power; he will not leave the guilty unpunished. His way is in the whirlwind and the storm, and clouds are the dust of his feet

1:7 The Lord is good, a refuge in times of trouble. He cares for those who trust in him

1:9 Whatever they plot against the Lord he will bring to an end; trouble will not come a second time

1:13 I will afflict you no more. Now I will break their yoke from your neck and tear your shackles away

HABAKKUK

2:4 See, he is puffed up; his desires are not upright—but the righteous will live by his faith

2:14 The earth will be filled with the knowledge of the glory of the Lord as the waters cover the sea

2:20 The Lord is in his holy temple; let all the earth be silent before him

3:2 Lord, I have heard of your fame; I stand in awe of your deeds, O Lord. Renew them in our day, in our time make them known; in wrath remember mercy

3:18-19 I will rejoice in the Lord, I will be joyful in God my Savior. The Sovereign Lord is my strength; he makes my feet like the feet of a deer, he enables me to go on the heights

ZEPHANIAH

3:12 I will leave within you the meek and humble, who trust in the name of Lord

3:17 The Lord your God is with you, he is mighty to save. He will take great delight in you, he will quiet you with his love, he will rejoice over you with singing

HAGGAI

2:5 This is what I covenanted with you when you when you came out of Egypt. And my Spirit remains among you. Do not fear

2:6-9 This is what the Lord Almighty says: 'In a little while I will once more shake the heavens and the earth, the sea and the dry land. I will shake all nations, and the desired of all nations will come, and I will fill this house with glory,' says the Lord Almighty. 'The silver is mine and the gold is mine,' declares the Lord Almighty. 'The glory of this present house will be greater than the glory of the former house,' says the Lord Almighty. 'And in this place I will grant peace,' declares the Lord Almighty

ZECHARIAH

1:3 This is what the Lord Almighty says: 'Return to me,' declares the Lord Almighty, 'and I will return to you,' says the Lord Almighty

1:16 This is what the Lord says, 'I will return to Jerusalem with mercy, and there my house will be rebuilt. And the measuring line will be stretched out over Jerusalem,' declares the Lord Almighty

2:4-5 'Jerusalem will be a city without walls because of the great number of men and livestock in it. And I myself will be a wall of fire around it,' declares the Lord, 'and I will be its glory within'

2:8 Whoever touches you touches the apple of his eye

2:10-13 'Shout and be glad, O Daughter of Zion. For I am coming, and I will live among you,' declares the Lord. 'Many nations will be joined with the Lord in that day and will become my people. I will live among you and you will know that the Lord Almighty has sent me to you. The Lord will inherit Judah as his portion in the holy land and will again choose Jerusalem. Be still before the Lord, all mankind, because he has roused himself from his holy dwelling'

4:6 'Not by might nor by power, but by my Spirit,' says the Lord Almighty

8:3 This is what the Lord says: 'I will return to Zion and dwell in Jerusalem. Then Jerusalem will be called The City of Truth, and the mountain of the Lord Almighty will be called The Holy Mountain'

8:7 I will bring them back to live in Jerusalem; they will be my people, and I will be faithful and righteous to them as their God

9:9-10 Rejoice greatly, O Daughter of Zion! Shout, daughter of Jerusalem! See, your king comes to you, righteous and having salvation, gentle and riding on a donkey, on a colt, the foal of a donkey. . . . He will proclaim peace to the nations. His rule will extend from sea to sea and from the River to the ends of the earth

12:10 I will pour out on the house of David and the inhabitants of Jerusalem a spirit of grace and supplication. They will look on me, the one they have pierced, and mourn for him as one mourns for an only child, and grieve bitterly for him as one grieves for a firstborn son

14:4-5 On that day his feet will stand on the Mount of Olives, east of Jerusalem, and the Mount of Olives will be split in two from east to west. . . . Then the Lord my God will come, and all the holy ones with him

14:9 The Lord will be king over the whole earth. On that day there will be one Lord, and his name the only name

MALACHI

1:11 'My name will be great among the nations, from the rising to the setting of the sun. In every place incense and pure offerings will be brought to my name, because my name will be great among the nations,' says the Lord Almighty

3:1-3 'See, I will send my messenger, who will prepare the way before me. Then suddenly the Lord you are seeking will come to his temple; the messenger of the covenant, whom you desire, will come,' says the Lord Almighty. But who can endure the day of his coming? Who can stand when he appears? For he will be like a refiner's fire or a launderer's soap. He will sit as a refiner and purifier of silver; he will purify the Levites and refine them like gold and silver

3:6 I the Lord do not change. So you, O descendants of Jacob, are not destroyed

3:7 'Return to me, and I will return to you,' says the Lord Almighty

4:2 For you who revere my name, the sun of righteousness will rise with healing in its wings. And you will go out and leap like calves released from the stall.

WHY ARE THE PROMISES NOT MANIFESTING IN MY LIFE?

God tells us to apply wisdom and instruction to our hearts. This is another way of communicating the concept of writing on the tablets of our hearts. All of these promises are true and we are qualified in Christ but they do not magically appear in our lives. God is not withholding any good thing from us so why are we not consistently experiencing his promises?

Jesus teaches us the mystery of experiencing this manifestation in Mark 4. He says the kingdom works as a seed and the condition of our heart determines the degree to which that seed will produce a harvest in our lives.

Believers have been given a new heart, a heart like his so it's not a matter of your heart being wicked, it's a matter of unbelief in your heart. I am not saying you don't have enough faith. Faith simply means to think to be true. Faith is to be persuaded of something. You have enough faith but sometimes your faith is more persuaded of lack or lies than it is of God's promises.

We are to focus on Jesus, giving him glory and honor for his victorious resurrection and triumph over all things. As we behold him we are to see ourselves in him. As we see ourselves in him we will begin to repent (change our perspective), renew our minds and experience transformation.

Promises do not come as a reward for your great faith, they are a byproduct of your transformation in Christ which comes from renewing your mind. Putting on the new man, the man created after God in true holiness and righteousness, is a process we do in our hearts and souls.

These promises and new creation realities are already true for Christ believers, we just do not allow ourselves to experience renewal and transformation in our inward man to the degree that these promises manifest. Meditation on the eternal truth of God, revealed in these promises, is the key to experiencing manifestation. They're already true, the seed has been planted because Christ is in you, now rest in these truths confidently and patiently, fully expecting manifestation.

As you meditate on each and every promise, do not allow doubt or carnal situations to invalidate the truth in each promise. Choose to believe that God has told you the truth and you are going to take him at his word, no matter what.

God keeps his promises, he is faithful to the end. Now stand firm and see the salvation of the Lord become fully established in your life!

ABOUT THE AUTHOR

Clint is the founding and lead pastor of Forward Church in Sharpsburg, GA. www.forward.church

Visit Clint's website for free messages and encouraging articles. www.clintbyars.com

Clint has developed powerful **Tools for Transformation**, including prayer and meditation resources designed to help you establish your heart in your identity in Christ and experience transformation. Access these Tools for Transformation at www.clintbyars.com.

OTHER BOOKS BY CLINT BYARS

Devil Walk: A True Story

Good God

Good News

The Watchers Chronicle Series: Books 1, 2 & 3

71233605R00057

Made in the USA
Columbia, SC
25 August 2019